Taming the Heterogeneity: Building Reliable Link Repositories for the Web of Data

Sanjay

CONTENTS

INTRODUCTION AND MOTIVATION

The Linked Data concept is well known as a collection of best practices to publish and connect structured web-based data. However, the number of available datasets has been growing significantly over the last decades [BHBL11]. Those datasets represent now the well known as Web of Data, which represent a large collection of concise and detailed interlinked data sets from multiple domains with large datasets [SPN+13a]. Thus, linking entries across heterogeneous data sources such as databases or knowledge bases, becomes an increasingly difficult p roblem [VSN17b; N A11b; S NPR18]. However, connections between datasets play a leading role in significant activities such as cross-ontology question answering [LUSM09], large-scale inferences [UKM+10] and data integration [Rah16]. In Linked Data, the Linksets are well known for executing the task of generating links between datasets [NA11b]. Due to the heterogeneity of the datasets, this uniqueness is reflected in the dataset's structure, making a challenging task to find r elations a mong t hose d atasets, i .e., t o identify how similar they are. In this way, we can say that Linked Data involves Datasets and Linksets and those Linksets needs to be maintained. There are many ways to maintain Linksets; one of those is to create a semantic web link repository, i.e., LinkLion [NSNR14a].

The current drawbacks addressed on this book are: Identifying and querying datasets from a huge heterogeneous collection of RDF datasets, in order to execute this task we need to know how the datasets are related and how similar they are, also the consistency of those datasets. After a brief explanation about what is involved in semantic web link repositories, we present and discuss the need for improvements on semantic web link repositories related to how the datasets are related and how similar they are, Identifying and querying those datasets, and assure the consistency of those repositories. Finally, a short introduction of each of the chapters is provided.

The following content shows the motivation where the research questions were originated and the related chapters.

1.1 THE NEED FOR IDENTIFYING AND QUERYING LOD DATASETS

One of the Semantic Web foundations is the possibility to dereference URIs to let applications negotiate their semantic content. However, this exploitation is often infeasible as the availability of such information depends on the reliability of networks, services, and human factors. Moreover, it has been shown that around 90% of the information published as Linked Open Data Linked Open Data (LOD) is available as data dumps and more than 60% of endpoints are offline. To this end, there is a need for a service to **identify** which dataset a URI were defined in order to let Linked Data consumers find the respective RDF data source, in case such information cannot be retrieved from the URI alone.

In order to **query** such amount of LOD datasets various interfaces such as LOD Stats[ADML12], LOD Laudromat[BRB+14], SPARQL endpoints provide access to the hundered of thousands of RDF datasets, representing billions of facts. These datasets are available in different formats such as raw data dumps and HDT files or directly accessible via SPARQL endpoints. Querying such large amount of distributed data is particularly challenging and many of these datasets cannot be directly queried using the SPARQL query language. To deal with such problems we present WIMU[VSN+18] and wimuQ[VSS19] covered on the respected chapters 4.1 and 6.

1.2 THE NEED FOR CONSISTENCY OF SEMANTIC WEB LINKED REPOSITORIES

More than 500 million facts on the Linked Data Web are statements across knowledge bases. The **consistency** of these links are of crucial importance for the Linked Data Web as they make a large number of tasks possible, including cross-ontology, question answering and federated queries. However, a large number of these links are erroneous and can thus lead to these applications producing absurd results. We present a time-efficient and complete approach for the detection of erroneous links for properties that are transitive[VAK15; VSN17a], covered with more details on the chapters 5.1 and 5.2.

1.3 THE NEED FOR RELATION AND INTEGRATION OF LOD DATASETS

Linking and integrating entries across heterogeneous data sources such as databases or knowledge bases, becomes an increasingly difficult problem, in particular w.r.t. the runtime of these tasks. Consequently, it is of utmost importance to provide time-efficient approaches for similarity joins in the Web of Data. While a number of scalable approaches have been developed there is not approach able to deal with such amount of datasets. In the web of data, there are several similar datasets, but there is no place that stores or provide such kind of information about how similar are the datasets, in our case, which attributes the datasets share. To this aim we create a this index[VSS20] to store the relation among them in order to see how similar they are based on their properties and classes[1], besides

---

1 Classes are also know as concepts

statistics about a large number of datasets, in which are covered in more details at chapters 4.3 and 4.2.

1.4 RESEARCH QUESTIONS AND CONTRIBUTIONS

For each motivation, we formulate a research question (RQ) towards the contribution of this book, Identifying, Relating, Consisting, and Querying Large Heterogeneous RDF Sources.

- (RQ1) How to Identify Datasets in Large Heterogeneous RDF Sources?
    - Covered in the chapter 4.1.
- (RQ2) How to create relations among a Large Amount of RDF Datasets?
    - Covered in the chapter 4.2.
- (RQ3) How to obtain Similar Resources Using String Similarity?
    - Covered in the chapter 4.3.
- (RQ4) How to tackle Heterogeneity in DBpedia Identifiers?
    - Covered in the chapter 5.1.
- (RQ5) How to Detect Erroneous Links in Large-Scale RDF Datasets?
    - Covered in the chapter 5.2.
- (RQ6) How to Query Large Heterogeneous RDF Datasets?
    - Covered in the chapter 6.

1.5 METHODOLOGY AND CONTRIBUTIONS

The figure 1 highlights the contributions of this book, which addresses problems pertaining to the need for identifying and querying LOD datasets, Consistency of semantic web Linked repositories, how LOD datasets are related and how similar they are, in which can also be visualized in the Linked Data Life-cycle [ALN11] (a simplification in three steps depicted in figure 1). In which the works DBpediaSameAs [VAK15] and CEDAL [VSN17a] are related to the **Classification, Evolution/Repair** and **Quality**. The works WIMU [VSN+18], wimuQ [VSS19], MFKC [VSN17b] and ReLOD [VSS20] are related to **Interlinking, Storage** and **Search/Browsing/Exploration**.

1. With WIMU[VSN+18] we address the RQ1, where we provide a regularly updated database index of more than 660K datasets from LODStats and LOD Laundromat, an efficient, low cost and scalable service on the web that shows which dataset most likely

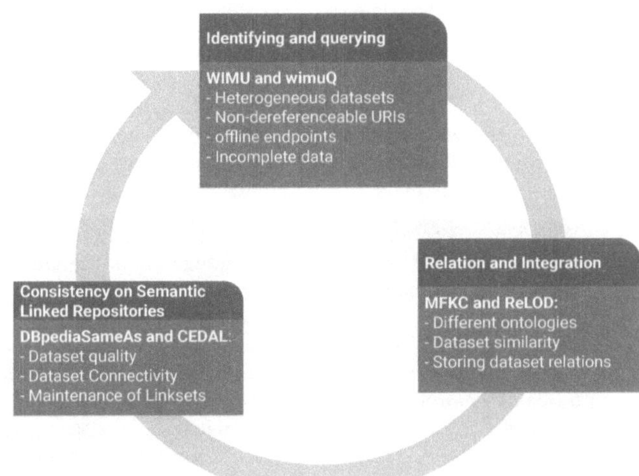

Figure 1: Contributions according to the Linked Data Life-cycle.

defines a URI and various statistics of datasets indexed from LODStats and LOD Laundromat. Covered in the **Chapter** 4.

2. With ReLOD[VSS20] we address the RQ2, which is a method to create a repository to store the similarity between a large number of datasets involving the detection of duplicated datasets and dataset chunks. To this aim, we store those similarities, providing an index to store the relation among them. The similarities processing is based on thee properties and classes of each dataset. We give a similarity score to each dataset pair and also provide an search engine to find similar datasets, classes and properties for a given a given dataset, class or property. We build the index over a total of 668,166 datasets from LOD Stats and LOD Laudromat as well as 559 active SPARQL endpoints. These data sources represent a total of 221.7 billion triples from more than 5 terabytes of information from datasets partially retrieved using the service "Where is My URI" (WIMU). Our evaluation on state-of-the-art real-data shows that more than 90% of datasets from LODLaundromat datasets are not using owl:equivalentProperty and owl:equivalentClass or other way to relate the data, reinforcing the need for a index of relations among LOD datasets. Covered in the **Chapter** 4.2.

3. With MKFC[VSN17b] we address the RQ3, in which is based in two nested filters, (1) First Frequency Filter and (2) Hash Intersection filter, that allow to discard candidates before calculating the actual similarity value, thus giving a considerable perfor-

mance gain, including the *k similarity filter* that allows detecting whether two strings s and t are similar in a fewer number of steps. We evaluate our approach with respect to its runtime and its scalability with several threshold settings and dataset sizes. Also, we present several parallel implementations of our approach and show that they work well on problems where $|D_s \times D_t| \geqslant 10^5$ pairs. Covered in the **Chapter** 4.3.

4. With DBpediaSameAs[VAK15] we address the RQ4, where it was described an approach for the mitigation of the identifier heterogeneity problem and implement a prototype where the user is able to evaluate existing links, as well as suggest new links to be rated. Together with the ability to generate statistics about good and bad links which, brings the possibility to have a quality control for the links to DBpedia. Also we define the DBpedia Unique Identifier (DUI), which instead of several transient `owl:sameAs` DBpedia URIs for the same final address, now is possible to have a unique URI from DBpedia. A DUI goes directly to the final address instead of having to process several possible intermediate results. Covered in the **Chapter** 5.1.

5. With CEDAL[VSN17a] we address the RQ5, where we present a time-efficient algorithm for the detection of erroneous links in large-scale link repositories without computing all closures required by the property axiom. An approach that brings the possibility to track the consistency problems inside link repositories, in which is a scalable algorithm that works well in a parallel and non-parallel mode. Together with a study case applied to a link repository called LinkLion and a new linkset quality measure based on the number of erroneous candidates. Covered in the **Chapter** 5.2.

6. With wimuQ[VSS19] we address the RQ6, where we present a hybrid SPARQL query processing engine which is able to retrieve results from 559 active SPARQL endpoints (with a total of 163.23 billion triples) and 668,166 datasets (with a total of 58.49 billion triples) from LOD Stats and LOD Laudromat. Thus, to the best of our knowledge, WimuQ is the first federated SPARQL query processing engine that executes SPARQL queries over a net total of 221.7 billion triples. As part of WimuQ, we present a low-cost API dubbed *SPARQL-a-lot* to execute SPARQL queries over LOD-a-lot [FBMPA17], a 300 GB HDT file of the LOD cloud. For the first time, to the best of our knowledge, we make use of the Concise Bounded Descriptions (CBDs) to execute federate SPARQL queries. We also make use of the WIMU index [VSN⁺18] to intelligently select the capable (also called relevant) [SNN14] data sources pertaining to the given SPARQL query. We evaluated our integrated

query engine on two real-data federated SPARQL querying benchmarks *LargeRDFBench* [SHN16],*FedBench* [SGH$^+$11] and one non-federated real data SPARQL benchmark selected from *FEASIBLE* [SMN15] benchmarks generation framework. Covered in the **Chapter** 6.

1.6 GENERAL USE CASES

As a motivation of our work, we describe distinct scenarios where the proposed book may be useful:

1.6.1 *The Heloise project*

The research network Heloise[RB16] in the field p rosopography[2] research, the research on large groups of persons, in History deals with a potential of more than 100 heterogeneous datasets with data related to historical persons. For collaboration on this research repositories the consortium proposed the Heloise Common Research Model (HCRM). One of the three layers Repository layer, Application layer and Research Interface layer, the Application layers deals with alignment and interlinking the repositories. The research project "Early Modern Professorial Career Patterns - Methodological research on online databases of academic history" is using the Heloise Methodology on a specific t opic o n C areer P atterns. A s a s imple example where Historians need to find o ut o n w hich U niversities professor "Levin Schücking" has been worked or taught. Therefore a federated request on all repositories has to be performed. This person is already presented on several RDF datasets for example:

The following questions are raised from this approach:

- Which datasets contain information about the person?

- Which datasets contain information about related research topics regarding career patterns ?

- Could result from different datasets complement the information about the research topic?

- Is the selected attribute represented in the same way in all datasets, if not what are the equivalent attributes in each dataset?

This case requires the user to know those more than 100 datasets in order to find the right attribute in each dataset, also what are the most relevant datasets. In this case, using part of the work in this book, i.e, WIMU[VSN$^+$18], the user will be able to know which datasets contain the given URI, in this case at least more 8 datasets founded by WIMU. With wimuQ[VSS19] which datasets are able to execute a query to obtain the information, and with ReLOD[AV20] to know what are the equivalent attributes by the similarity level.

More specific use cases are available inside the chapters 4.1, 4.2, 5.2 and 6, also an application case is available at the appendix 5.3.

1.7 CHAPTER OVERVIEW

On the **Chapter** 2 we introduce the basic concepts and notation that are necessary to understand the rest of this book. The notation presented in this chapter is used throughout the book. On the **Chapter** 3 we discuss the state-of-the-art research work related to this book. **Chapter** 4.1 is based on [VSN$^+$18] and introduces WIMU, a regularly updated database index of more than 660K datasets from LODStats and LOD Laundromat, an efficient, low cost and scalable service on the web that shows which dataset most likely defines a URI. **Chapter** 4.2 is based on [VSS20] a method to create a repository to store the similarity between a large number of datasets involving the detection of duplicated datasets and dataset chunks. **Chapter** 4.3 is based on [VSN17b] and presents two nested filters, (1) First Frequency Filter and (2) Hash Intersection filter, that allow to discard candidates before calculating the actual similarity value, thus giving a considerable performance gain. **Chapter** 5.1 is based on [VAK15] presenting an approach which improves the quality of Link repositories with a case applied to DBpedia, in which shows an approach for the mitigation of the identifier heterogeneity problem and implement a prototype where the user is able to evaluate existing links, as well as suggest new links to be rated. **Chapter** 5.2 is based on [VSN17a] present an extension of the previous work [VAK15] discussing the consistency of semantic web Linked repositories in a more wide point of view. **Chapter** 6 is based on [VSS19] and presents a hybrid SPARQL query processing engine which is able to retrieve results from a large number of heterogeneous LOD datasets. The approach is called WimuQ in which is the first federated SPARQL query processing engine that executes SPARQL queries over a net total of 221.7 billion triples. Finally, **chapter** 7 concludes this work and proposes some future work in related areas of research.

PRELIMINARIES

This chapter describes the main concepts used along of this work.

2.1 SEMANTIC WEB

The Semantic Web, or Web of Data, was proposed as an extension of the World Wide Web by [BLHL01] and consists of a huge amount of interlinked, machine-interpretable data. This provides the basis for complex information seeking tasks such as "Which hotels are near lakes with a water temperature of more than 20 Celsius in July?" The Web of Data is well suited to these tasks because it provides information that is interpretable by machines and semantically linked. The Semantic Web includes and extends, among others, the following standards and technologies:

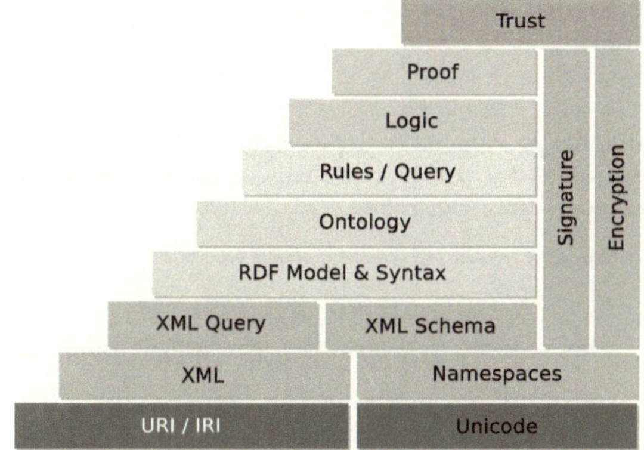

Figure 2: The Semantic Web Stack. Source:
`https://commons.wikimedia.org/wiki/File:W3c-semantic-web-layers.svg`

2.1.1 *URIs and URLs*

A Uniform Resource Identifier (URI) is a sequence of characters that uniquely identifies an abstract or physical resource [BLFM05]. To save space, URIs can be abbreviated using prefixes, see Tabelle 1. For example, can be abbreviated to `dbr:Berlin`.

A Uniform Resource Locator (URL) is a URI that contains a resource locator, which describes a way to access that resource [BLMM94].

Prefix	
rdf	
rdfs	
owl	
xsd	
dc	
dbo	
dbr	
dbp	

Table 1: URL prefixes used throughout this work.

2.1.2 *Linked Data*

While hypertext on the Web of Documents can contain hyperlinks to data, this data does not have hypertext capability itself. For example, you cannot link a row of a Comma-Separated Values (CSV) table to a row in another table. Another weakness of the World Wide Web (WWW) is the missing *semantics* of hyperlinks: they are untyped and thus do not provide machine-processable information about the kind of association a hyperlink represents. *Linked Data* [?] remedies those deficiencies using four rules:

1. Items of discourse are identified by URIs

2. Those URIs are also HTTP URLs, so that more information about a resource can be gained by *dereferencing* it using HTTP lookup.

3. Lookup results in information expressed using the standards Resource Description Framework (RDF) and SPARQL.

4. URIs are joined by typed links, so that related information can be discovered.

If Linked Data is published under an open license, it is called *Linked Open Data*.

LINKED OPEN DATA CLOUD   All data sets that are publicly available as Linked Data under an open licence and that are connected with other data sets, are collectively called the LOD cloud.

2.1.3 Resource Description Framework

RDF is a set of specifications[1] to describe arbitrary facts about *resources* (URIs[2]) as *triples*, see Definition 1. A set of triples is called an *(RDF) graph* in the context of querying RDF. A set of triples that describes a certain domain is also be called an *(RDF) knowledge base* and may be the union of multiple RDF graphs. RDF can be serialized in several formats, including *N-Triples* and *Turtle*. A graph database for RDF is called a *triple store*.

Definition 1 (RDF triple). *An (RDF) triple represents a single fact and consists of a subject, property (also called a* predicate*) and object. All elements of a triple can be a resource, but the object can also be a literal. Subject and object can also be blank nodes, anonymous resources with no URI, but they are not used in this work. Formally: Let U be a set of URIs, $U = IPC$, where I are the instances, P the properties and C the classes. Let $L \subset \sigma^*$ be a set of literals, where σ is the unicode alphabet. We define an RDF triple t as $t \in U \times P \times (UL)$.*

N-TRIPLES   Each line in an N-Triples file contains a single triple. Depending on the type of object, a triple is serialized in one of four ways:

```
1  <subject> <predicate> <object-resource>.
2  <subject> <predicate> "object-untyped-literal".
3  <subject> <predicate> "object-untyped-literal"@languagetag.
4  <subject> <predicate> "object-typed-literal"^^datatype.
```

The city of Berlin is represented in DBpedia [LIJ[+]14] as Dereferencing this URL and choos-ing the N-Triples format yields the following (excerpt, DBpedia ver-sion 2016-10):

The N-Triples format is easy to process in scripts because it is line-based but it is hard to read due to the verbosity.

---

1 see

2 Resources can also be IRIs, a superset of URIs with a wider range of allowed Unicode characters, but they are not used in this work.

TURTLE   Turtle is a superset of N-Triples with the added possibility of abbreviating URIs using prefixes as well as grouping together repeated subjects and subject-predicate pairs. The city of Berlin from DBpedia [LIJ$^+$14] is represented in Turtle as follows (excerpt, version 2016-10):

```
dbp:locatedIn  dbr:Germany;
dbp:areaCode  "030";
rdfs:label  "Berlin"@de, "Berlijn"@nl;
dbp:populationTotal "3610156"@xsd:integer.
```

From this point on, we use Turtle for all RDF listings because it is concise and easy to read. We also omit prefix declarations in Turtle code and refer to Tabelle 1. A prefix can be the empty string; We use this for generic examples and in the context of statements locally to a single knowledge base.

2.1.4 *Ontologies*

In computer science[3], an ontology is an explicit specification of a conceptualization [Gru93]. Ontologies are an active research area. A domain can be described in great detail using OWL [HKR09], but in the context of RDF Data Cube Question Answering (RDCQA), ontologies are mostly used as a lightweight schema that provides context to a large amount of instance data. For example, DBpedia [LIJ$^+$14] version 2016-04 contains 760 classes and 5044222 instances.

A *class* is a set of resources and can be defined either intrinsically or extrinsically. Intrinsically, a class is defined by the properties of its members. For example, a motor boat is a boat that has at least one motor. A member of a class is called its *instance*. Depending on the type of ontology, such an instance my be a class or property itself. An instance that is neither a class nor a property is also called an *individual*. In the context of RDCQA, however, classes are extrinsically defined, that is, the class membership is explicitly mentioned.

$$\text{City} = \big\{\text{Berlin}, \text{Leipzig}, \ldots, \text{London}\big\}$$

In RDF, class membership is stated using the property rdf:type, with the instance as the subject and the class as the object.

```
1  dbr:Berlin rdf:type dbo:City.
```

Because rdf:type is such a commonly used property, Turtle defines the shorthand a for it:

```
1  dbr:Berlin a dbo:City.
```

As classes are sets, they can be subclasses (subsets) or superclasses (supersets) of other classes.

$$\text{MotorBoat} \subseteq \text{Boat} \subseteq \text{Vehicle}$$

Multiple classes can share the same instance and a class can be a subclass of multiple superclasses:

```
1  :myBoat a :MotorBoat, SailBoat.
2  :MotorBoat rdfs:subClassOf :Boat.
3  :Boat rdfs:subClassOf :Vehicle.
```

Using the definition of a subset[4] and the transitivity[5] of the subset relation, superclass membership can be *inferred*[6], that is, it can be logically deduced. When answering questions like Which vehicles are powered by a motor?, a motor boat can be found even if it is defined as an instance of *MotorBoat* and not *Vehicle*. By providing additional correct answers, inferrence increases the recall, see ??.

The subclass relation may contain cycles, that is $C_1 \subseteq C_2 \subseteq \ldots \subseteq C_n \subseteq C_1$, but that is usually avoided as it implies the equivalence of all involved classes.

2.2 RDF GRAPH

An RDF graph is a set of RDF triples which has a set of subjects and objects of triples in the graph called nodes. Given an infinite set U of URIs, an infinite set B of blank nodes and an infinite set of literals L, a RDF triple is a triple $\langle s, p, o \rangle$ where the subject $s \in (U \cup B)$, the predicate $p \in U$ and the object $o \in (U \cup B \cup L)$. An RDF triple represents an assertion of a "piece of knowledge", so if the triple $\langle s, p, o \rangle$ exists, then, the logical assertion $p(s, o)$ holds true. An RDF graph is also represented by a collection of RDF triples and it can be seen as a set of statements describing, partially or completely, a certain knowledge.

2.3 TRANSITIVE PROPERTY

A transitive property is defined by: $\forall a, b, c \in X : (p(a, b) \wedge p(b, c)) \implies p(a, c)$, where p represents a relation between two elements of a set X.

---

4 $A \subseteq B \Leftrightarrow \forall a \in A : a \in B$

5 $A \subseteq B \subseteq C \Rightarrow A \subseteq C$

6 Inference requires support by the query engine, addition of the extra triples to the knowledge base or support by the Semantic Question Answering (SQA) system.

2.4 EQUIVALENCE

An equivalence relation is a binary relation that is reflexive, symmetric and transitive. According to OWL semantics, `owl:sameAs` is an equivalence relation.

2.5 LINKSET

According to the W3C,[7] a linkset is a collection of RDF links between two datasets. It is a set of RDF triples in which all subjects are in one dataset and all objects are in another dataset. RDF links often have the `owl:sameAs` predicate, but any other property could occur as the predicate as well. Formally, according to [ACHZo9], a linkset LS is a set of RDF triples where for all triples $t_i = \langle s_i, p_i, o_i \rangle \in$ LS, the subject is in one dataset, i.e. all s_i are described in S, and the object is in another dataset, i.e. all o_i are described in T, where S and T are datasets. We use the word *linkset* for either RDF knowledge base files and dump files from RDF link repositories.

2.6 RDF GRAPH PARTITIONING

Given a graph $G = (V, E, lbl, L)$, a graph partitioning, C, is a division of V into k partitions $P_1, P_2, ..., P_k$ such that $\bigcup_{1 \leqslant i \leqslant k} P_i = V$, and $P_i \cap P_j = \emptyset$ for any $i \neq j$. The edge cut E_c is the set of edges whose vertices belong to different partitions, $lbl : E \cup V \rightarrow L$ is a labeling function, and L is a set of labels.

The definition comes from a recent survey about RDF graph partitioning [TSW15].

2.7 BASIC GRAPH PATTERN

A Basic Graph Pattern (BGP)[8] is represented by a set of Triple Patterns[Fleo8].

2.8 RDF DATASET

An RDF dataset is a set:

$G, (< u_1 >, G_1), (< u_2 >, G2), ... (< u_n >, G_n)$

where G and each G_i are graphs, and each <u_i> is an IRI. Each <u_i> is distinct. G is called the default graph. (<u_i>, G_i) are called named graphs.

———————————————————————

GraphPatterns

2.9   SPARQL

SPARQL Protocol and RDF Query Language (SPARQL) is the language to query RDF datasets, in which the formal definition of a SPARQL Query is: A SPARQL Abstract Query is a tuple (E, D, R) where E is a SPARQL algebra expression, D is an RDF Dataset and R is a query form.

2.10   FEDERATED QUERIES

Federated Queries have the aim to collect information from more than one datasets is of central importance for many semantic web and linked data applications [SKI$^+$13; SKI$^+$14]. One of the key step in federated query processing is the *source selection*. The goal of the source selection is to find relevant sources (i.e., datasets) for the given user query.

3

In order to give an overview of the state of the art, the figure 3, the tables 2 and 3 shows the selected works relating the content with the four topics of this book, i.e., Identifying, Relating, Consisting and Querying Large Heterogeneous RDF sources. More details are presented in the following sections.

This chapter discusses the state-of-the-art research work related to this boo

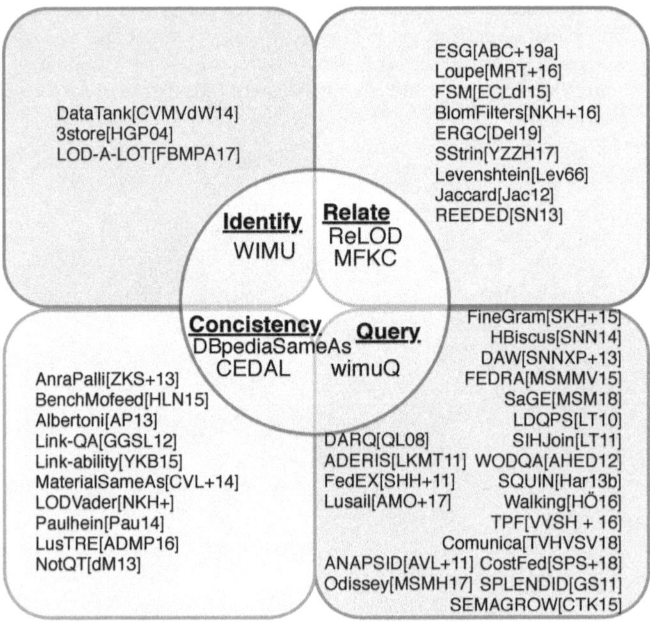

Figure 3: State of the art in a Venn Diagram.

Table 2: State of the art overview of Resources (R), Methodologies (M) and Benchmark (B) regarding to Identifying (Identify), Relating (Relation), Consisting (Consistency) and Querying (Query) Large Heterogeneous RDF Sources

Approach	Identify	Relation	Consistency	Query
DataTank[CVMVdW14]	R	-	-	-
3store[HGP04]	R	-	-	-
LOD-A-LOT [FBMPA17]	R	-	-	-
ESG[ABC+19a]	-	M	-	-
Loupe[MRT+16]	-	R	-	-
FSM[ECLdI15]	-	R	-	-
BlomFilters[NKH+16]	-	R	-	-
ERGC[Del19]	-	M	-	-
SStrin[YZZH17]	-	R	-	-
Levenshtein[Lev66]	-	R	-	-
Jaccard[Jac12]	-	R	-	-
REEDED[SN13]	-	R	-	-
AnraPalli[ZKS+13]	-	-	M	-
BenchMofeed[HLN15]	-	-	B	-
Albertoni[AP13]	-	-	M	-
Link-QA[GGSL12]	-	-	R	-
Link-ability[YKB15]	-	-	M	-
MaterialSameAs[CVL+14]	-	-	M	-
LODVader[NKH+]	-	-	M	-
Paulhein[Pau14]	-	-	M	-
LusTRE[ADMP16]	-	-	R	-
NotQT[dM13]	-	-	M	-
DARQ[QL08]	-	-	-	R
ADERIS[LKMT11]	-	-	-	R
FedEX[SHH+11]	-	-	-	B
Lusail[AMO+17]	-	-	-	R

Table 3: Continuation of table 2

Approach	Identify	Relation	Consistency	Query
SPLENDID[GS11]	-	-	-	R
CostFed[SPS$^+$18]	-	-	-	B
ANAPSID[AVL$^+$11]	-	-	-	R
SEMAGROW[CTK15]	-	-	-	R
Odissey[MSMH17]	-	-	-	R
FineGram[SKH$^+$15]	-	-	-	M
HBiscus[SNN14]	-	-	-	R
DAW[SNNXP$^+$13]	-	-	-	R
FEDRA[MSMMV15]	-	-	-	R
SaGE[MSM18]	-	-	-	R
LDQPS[LT10]	-	-	-	R
SIHJoin[LT11]	-	-	-	R
WODQA[AHED12]	-	-	-	R
SQUIN[Har13b]	-	-	-	R
Walking[HÖ16]	-	-	-	M
TPF[VVSH$^+$16]	-	-	-	R
Comunica[TVHVSV18]	-	-	-	R
WIMU[AMO$^+$17]	R/M	-	-	-
wimuQ[AMO$^+$17]	-	-	-	R/M
MFKC[AMO$^+$17]	-	R/M	-	-
ReLOD[AMO$^+$17]	-	R/M	-	-
CEDAL[AMO$^+$17]	-	-	R/M	-
DBpediaSameAs[AMO$^+$17]	-	-	R	-

3.1 IDENTIFYING DATASETS IN LARGE HETEROGENEOUS RDF SOURCES

The State-of-the-art of Identifying LOD datasets is presented in the following and highlighting the differences with our approach, in which the table 4 highlights the main points.

Table 4: State of the art overview of Resources (R), Methodologies (M) and
Benchmark (B) regarding to RESTful service (RS), Avaibility (AV),
Queryble Index (QI), Dataset Provenance (DP), Largest Linked Data
hubs (LD) and Ranked Score URI-Dataset (RU)

Approach	RS	AV	QI	DP	LD	RU
DataTank[CVMVdW14]	yes	yes	yes	no	no	no
3store[HGP04]	no	no	yes	no	no	no
LOD-A-LOT [FBMPA17]	no	yes	yes	no	yes	no
WIMU [VSN$^+$18]	yes	yes	yes	yes	yes	yes

The work presented in [CVMVdW14] shows how to set up a Linked
Data repository called *DataTank* and publish data as turtle files or
through a SPARQL endpoint. The difference with WIMU is that we
provide a RESTful service instead of a setup to configure a Linked
Data repository.

The work in [HGP04] is based on an approach developed for the
3store RDF triple store and describes a technique for indexing RDF
documents allowing the rank and retrieval of their contents. Their
index contained 10^7 triples, which was remarkable for the early years
of the Semantic Web. Moreover, their system is not available for tests
anymore. A similar point here is that the authors claim that for a
given URI from an RDF document, the system will retrieve the URLs
of documents containing that URI.

In the approach called LOD-A-LOT [FBMPA17] which is a
queryable dump file of the LOD Cloud[1], there are some differences
with WIMU. The first, it is not possible to know the provenance of
the URI in order to know which dataset the URI was defined. They
provide a huge dump file[2] containing all the data from LOD Laundromat[3]. LOD Laundromat itself provides an endpoint to an inverted index of their data[4]. However, finding the original document a URI was
defined in is not trivial, as the returned metadata only describe the
datasets themselves [BRB$^+$14]. Moreover, as the primary aim of LOD
Laundromat is to "clean" Linked Data, most dumps are possibly not
continuously monitored, once cleaned.

Comparing with all the approaches above, the main advantage of
WIMU is that the datasets a URI likely belongs to are ranked using a
score. Our index has also a larger coverage, as it includes data from

the two largest Linked Data hubs, i.e., LODStats [ADML12] and LOD Laundromat [BRB⁺14], and the most updated SPARQL endpoints. Finally, WIMU is able to process RDF files containing more than one URI at the same time[5].

3.2 RELATING LARGE AMOUNT OF RDF DATASETS

The table 6 summarize the works with aim of relating Large amount of RDF datasets.

Table 6: State of the art overview regarding to Relating Large amount of RDF datasets, withing the following characteristics: Compute similarity level among the datasets based on the properties and class similarities (Sim), Large amount of Data (LAD), Identify duplicated data (IDP)

Approach	Sim	LAD	IDP
ESG [ABC⁺19a]	no	yes	no
Loupe [MRT⁺16]	no	no	no
FSM [ECLdI15]	yes	no	no
BloomFilters [NKH⁺16]	no	no	yes
MFKC [VSN17b]	yes	no	no
ReLOD [AV20]	yes	yes	yes

The work from [ABC⁺19a; ABC⁺19b; ABC⁺19c] contains very important statistics about LOD datasets, including a data structure called Equivalence Set Graph (ESG), which allows specifying compact views of large RDF graphs thus easing the accomplishment of statistical observations like the number of concepts defined in a graph. The work helps to show that the LOD datasets are not really linked and the **main difference** here is that they do not have a goal to compute similarity level among the datasets based on the properties and class similarities.

Loupe [MRT⁺16] has an index of property and classes from some datasets, but still fewer datasets and it is not incremental.

The approach from [ECLdI15] it is built on the assumption that similar datasets should have a similar structure and include semantically similar resources and relationships based on the combination of Frequent Subgraph Mining (FSM) techniques, used to synthesize the datasets and find similarities among them.

The works from [NKH+16] and [BNKK+17] also provides an approach to identify duplicated data in huge datasets from LODLaundromat and DBpedia. A good point to highlight in those works is the use of bloom filters, which helps to identify duplicated data. The identified different aims compared with our approach are an index of similarity of the datasets based on properties and classes shared among them and the identification of datasets to execute a given SPARQL query.

We should also consider the enforcement from Entity Reconciliation Community Group (ERCG)[6], in which aim to document an existing API, share the experiences and lessons learned from it[Del19].

Those works cover an important relationship but none of them look into our main drawback here, which is to obtain the similarity level among a huge amount of datasets.

3.2.1 *Obtaining Similar Resources using String Similarity*

Our approach[VSN17b] can be considered an extension of the state-of-the-art algorithm introduced in [SAAM14], which describes a string-based distance function (SDF) based on string hashing [SM13; Riv92]. The naive approach of MFKC [SAAM14] is a metric for string comparison built on a hash function, which gets a string and outputs the most frequent two characters with their frequencies. This algorithm was used for text mining operations. The approach can be divided into two parts: (1) The hashing function is applied to both input strings, where the output is a string that contains the two most frequent characters; the first and third elements keep the characters and second and fourth elements keep the frequency of these characters. (2) The hashes are compared, where will return a real number between 0 and lim. By default $lim = 10$, since the probability of having ten occurrences of the two most frequent characters in common between two strings is low. If the output of the function is 10, this case indicates that there is no common character and any value below 10 means there are some common characters shared among the strings.

Our work is similar to the one presented in [YZZH17], which features a parallel processing framework for string similarity using filters to avoid unnecessary comparisons.

Among the several types of string similarity, emerging works have been done for measures such as Levenshtein-distance [Lev66], which is a string distance function that calculates the minimum number of edit operations (i.e., delete, insert or update) to transform the first into the second string. The Jaccard Index [Jac12], also called Jaccard coefficient, works on the bitwise operators, where the strings are treated at

---

6 Link to the official web page of the Entity Reconciliation Community Group

bit level. REEDED [SN13] was the first approach for the time-efficient execution of weighted edit distances.

3.3   CONSISTENCY ON LARGE AMOUT OF RDF SOURCES

This section covers the state of the art regarding the consistency on Large amount of RDF sources, in which the table 8 summarizes the main points, and more detais are given in the following sections.

Table 8: State of the art overview regarding to Consistency on Large amount of RDF datasets, withing the following characteristics: Allow manual validation (MV), Rate the links (RL), Linkset completeness (LC), Graph partitions (GP), Larger Linksets with more than 19 million triples (LL), Provenance of the Links(PL), Error Classification (EC)

Approach	MV	RL	LC	GP	LL	PL	EC
BenchMofeed [HLN15]	yes	no	no	no	no	no	no
sameAs.org [GJM09]	no	no	no	no	no	no	no
DBpediaSameAs [VAK15]	yes	yes	no	no	no	no	no
AlbertoniLink [AP13]	no	no	yes	no	no	no	no
LinkQA [GGSL12]	no	no	yes	no	no	no	no
LinkAbility [YKB15]	no	no	yes	no	no	no	no
MateriaLink [CVL$^+$14]	no	no	yes	no	no	no	no
LODVader [NKH$^+$]	no	yes	yes	no	no	no	no
PaulheimLink [Pau14]	no	yes	yes	no	no	no	no
LusTRE [ADMP16]	no	yes	yes	no	no	no	no
MeloLinks [dM13]	no	yes	yes	no	no	no	no
CEDAL [VSN17a]	yes	no	yes	yes	yes	yes	yes

3.3.1   *Heterogeneity in DBpedia Identifiers*

The state of the art of the work presented in [VAK15] is based on the work [ZKS$^+$13], in which elaborates a data quality assessment methodology in DBpedia, which comprises of a manual and semi-automatic process. This work drive us to a reinforcement about the concept of data quality used in our work, when in our case will be more a manual process and also we are able to improve the DBpedia data quality.

The work [HLN15], presents a two staged experiment for the creation of gold standards that act as benchmarks for several interlinking algorithms. The similar aspects of this works are: The validation of links and a dubbed manual validation, where the user i.e. validator or evaluator specifies whether a link generated by an interlinked tool is correct or incorrect. The results of the link validation process are used to learn presumably better link specifications and thus achieving high-quality. Also, this work proposes an experiment to investigate the effect of user intervention in dataset interlinking on small knowledge bases.

A related problem with sameAs.org

The sameAs.org[GJM09] is a service that leading source of co-reference data on the Semantic Web. For example, when the web site sameAs.org is accessed with a URI from Freebase that should bring information about a country called Brazil.

Was used the URI (`http://rdf.freebase.com/ns/m.015fr`) as parameter to the service, and is received as return more than 1140 URIs as shown in figure 4, but the user can have a doubt about which one is the correct.

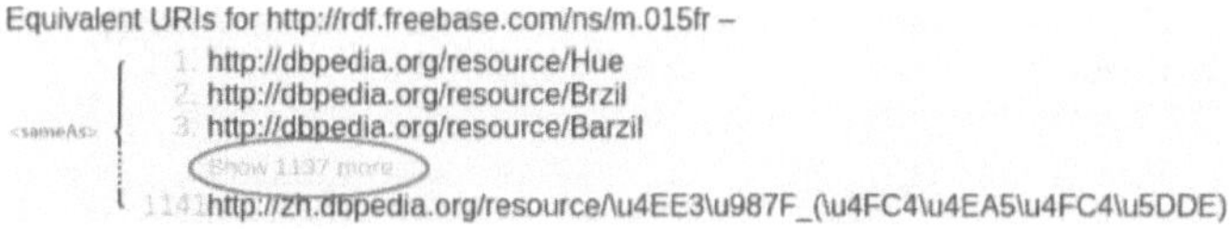

Equivalent URIs for http://rdf.freebase.com/ns/m.015fr –

<sameAs>
1. http://dbpedia.org/resource/Hue
2. http://dbpedia.org/resource/Brzil
3. http://dbpedia.org/resource/Barzil
Show 1137 more
1141 http://zh.dbpedia.org/resource/\u4EE3\u987F_(\u4FC4\u4EA5\u4FC4\u5DDE)

Figure 4: Several URIs with the property `owl:sameAs` from the web site sameAs.org.

This part of our work[VAK15] is not an alternative to the sameAs web site, but brings possibilities, like, was noticed that the `http://sameAs.org` does not provide a way to rate the link, but with this rating, is possible to improve the quality of the data, and bring some facility to the user.

3.3.2 *Detection of Erroneous Links in Large-Scale RDF Datasets*

This part of our work[VSN17a] has the aim of detecting erroneous links in large-scale link repositories improving the consistency. The state-of-the-art include the following related works:

ALBERTONI ET AL. [AP13]   focus on the quality dimension of completeness using scoring functions and also introduce a notion of linkset quality, considering only `owl:sameAs`. The work proposes three quality indicators to assess completeness. The extension of this work [ADMP15] focuses on `skos:exactMatch` linksets and a multilingual gain.

THE LINK-QA TOOL [GGSL12]   uses two network measures designed for Linked Data (i.e., open `sameAs` chains, and description richness) and three classic network measures (i.e., degree, centrality, clustering coefficient) in order to determine whether a set of links can improve the quality of linked data.

DBPEDIASAMEAS [VAK15]   is a work in which Transitive Redirects Links are redundancies at DBpedia that supposes a link to the same place, in other words, they use the `owl:sameAs` property. These links will redirect other links, to provide a transition between the links, hence the name transitive. In this case, instead of using the transitive links that point to the same final destination URI, the final URI is used directly.

THE WORK PROPOSED IN [YKB15]   is a metric-driven approach for interlinking assessment of a single dataset. It introduces the concept of *link-ability*, which shows the potential of a dataset being linked from other datasets, and in general, assesses whether a dataset is good to be interlinked with another dataset using three groups of metrics.

THE APPROACH AT [CVL⁺14]   proposes strategies in order to reduce the cognitive overhead of creating materialized `owl:sameAs` linksets and to correctly maintain them using two types of components that triple stores should include, which would improve the support for materialized `owl:sameAs` linksets in the creation and maintenance stages.

THE WORK FROM [NKH⁺]   evaluates the quantity of links between distributions, datasets, and ontologies categorizing and defining different types of links using probabilistic data structures. The results show valid links, dead links, and a number of namespaces described by distributions and datasets. The analysis was conducted using LODVader [BNMB⁺16]. An important point here and in works such as [SLZ09; BRB⁺14; Mäk14] is that they do not mention or use any quality dimension as defined in some important works such as [ZRM⁺15; ADMP15]; moreover, they do not consider the axioms related to the properties. The quality is given solely by the number of links between datasets.

THE WORK DESCRIBED IN [PAU14]   covers an unsupervised approach for finding erroneous links, in which each link is represented as a feature vector in a higher dimensional vector space, and finds wrong links by means of different multi-dimensional outliers.

THE W3C   has a vocabulary to express the quality of data, including a linkset[7], that is based on the survey by Zaveri et al. [ZRM+15].

THE WORK DESCRIBED IN [ADMP16]   discuss results of quality evaluation on linksets created using a framework called LusTRE with two quality measures, the *average linkset reachability* and the *average linkset importing*. Similar to CEDAL, this work realizes that the research on Linked Data quality has been mainly focused on datasets, not on linksets. However, they focus on the SKOS[8] vocabulary, more precisely skos:exactMatch linksets, and the experiments from CEDAL were processed in large scale link repositories with more than 10^7 triples, not only $31,298$ triples.

THE WORK DESCRIBED IN [DM13]   provides an algorithm with the intention to mitigate the problem of constraints violations in sameAs links automatically. Our approach has some different characteristics, such as CEDAL provides a classification of errors and show that some of them cannot be dealt with automatically in an accurate way, CEDAL use graph partitions in which scales better than this existing approach. This is also shown by the evaluation of CEDAL on larger datasets (19 million vs 3 million), CEDAL preserves the provenance of the links, CEDAL does not remove automatically constraints violations due to the fact that the output results involves semantic accuracy and thus needs human feedback. The similarities include the fact that we also focus on owl:sameAs and we reveal a significant amount of sameAs links that do not adhere to the strict semantics of the OWL standard and hence do not reflect genuine identity.

INTERLINKING EDUCATIONAL RESOURCES[RSSA15; DSAE+13; DYG+12]   , is an effort to interlinking educational resources into linked data standards, but without taking care of the problem of the consistency of the linksets.

THE WORK PRESENTED IN [DAD13]   is a research note about a study of available web datasets related to education. They focus in a network of educational web data. The common point is that part of the analysis is about of owl:sameAs links from education area and the novelty of our work is about we are taking care about linksets and not only datasets.

THERE IS A STUDY MORE GENERIC AND COMPREHENSIVE ABOUT LINKED DATA FOR SCIENCE IN GENERAL AND EDUCATION [KDD13] , in which makes an introductory analysis of four papers documenting the most recent developments in Linked Data for Science and Education.

THE WORK FROM [RCVGAP+12] present a study about Information and Communication Technologies (ICT) tools to support learning activities with a Linked Data approach for the discovery of educational ICT tools in the Web of Data, in which proposes to collect data from third-party sources, align it to a vocabulary understandable by educators and finally publish it to be consumed by educational applications. The relation here is the effort to turn educational data in linked data and improve the quality.

THE WORK [ZFR11] has the aim of introduce the current efforts toward the release and exploitation of The Open University's (OU) Linked Open Data (LOD) referring to production and consumption. The relation here is about bring some improvement to the educational linked data, but without taking care of quality of linksets.

COMMON POINTS AMONG THESE EXISTING WORKS are the improvement and maintenance of link repositories. Aspects include the use of scoring functions, transitive and redirect links, metrics for interlinking datasets, probabilistic data structures, vector space models, and the creation of standards. Our approach provides a high-performance way to dealing with heterogeneous knowledge bases showing the provenance and detecting inconsistent links in large-scale link repositories. Although our work bears some resemblance to existing work on detecting erroneous link candidates in large link repositories, none of the above has considered evaluating the consistency of equivalence relations using a data quality measure.

The novelty of CEDAL with respect to the state-of-the-art can be enumerated in five points. Our approach (1) uses graph partitions and hence scales better than existing approaches using closures, (2) can be applied to larger linksets, with more than 19 million triples, (3) preserves the provenance of the links, (4) shows that some of the error classifications cannot be dealt with automatically in an accurate way and (5) does not remove automatically constraints violations due to the fact that the output results involves semantic accuracy and thus needs human feedback.

3.4 QUERYING LARGE HETEROGENEOUS RDF DATASETS

In this section, we provide a brief overview of the state-of-the-art pertaining to querying a huge amount of heterogeneous LOD datasets, in which we start with approaches for federated query processing. The table 10 summarizes the main points.

Table 10: State of the art overview regarding to Querying Large Heterogeneous RDF Datasets, withing the following characteristics: SPARQL query federation (SQF), Link Traversal based SPARQL federation (LTF), Dataset Identification (DI), Source Selection (SS), Duplicate Aware (DA)

Approach	SQF	LTF	DI	SS	DA
DARQ [QL08]	yes	no	no	yes	no
ADERIS [LKMT11]	yes	no	no	yes	no
FedEx [SHH+11]	yes	no	no	yes	no
Lusail [AMO+17]	yes	no	no	yes	no
SPLENDID [GS11]	yes	no	no	yes	no
CostFed [SPS+18]	yes	no	no	yes	no
ANAPSID [AVL+11]	yes	no	no	yes	no
SEMAGrow [CTK15]	yes	no	no	yes	no
Odissey [MSMH17]	yes	no	no	yes	no
Mulder [EGL+18]	yes	no	no	yes	no
DAW [SNNXP+13]	yes	no	no	yes	yes
Fedra [MSMMV15]	yes	no	no	yes	yes
SaGe [MSM18]	yes	no	no	yes	no
LDQPS [LT10]	yes	yes	no	yes	no
SIHJoin [LT11]	yes	yes	no	yes	no
WoDQA [AHED12]	yes	yes	no	yes	no
SQUIN [Har13b]	yes	yes	no	yes	yes
TPF [VVSH+16]	yes	yes	no	yes	yes
Comunica [TVHVSV18]	yes	yes	no	yes	yes
wimuQ [VSS19]	yes	yes	yes	yes	yes

query federation over multiple sparql endpoints: DARQ [QL08], ADERIS [LKMT11], FedX [SHH+11], Lusail [AMO+17], SPLENDID [GS11], CostFed [SPS+18], ANAPSID [AVL+11], SemaGrow [CTK15], Odyssey [MSMH17], and MULDER [EGL+18] are examples of state-of-the-art SPARQL endpoint federation engines. These approaches can be further divided into 3 categories namely *index-only*, *index-free*, and hybrid (index+ASK) approaches [SKH+15].

DARQ and ADERIS are examples of the *index-only* SPARQL query federation approaches over multiple SPARQL endpoints. DARQ implements a cardinality-based query planner with bind join implementation in nested loops. ADERIS is an adaptive query engine that implements a cost-based query planner. It also makes use of the index-based nested loop join.

FedX and Lusail are examples of the *index-free* query federation approaches over multiple SPARQL endpoints. FedX only makes use of ASK queries for source selection. It implements a heuristic-based query planner. Comparing to DARQ, the number of endpoints requests is greatly reduced by using bind joins in a block nested loop fashion [SHH+11]. A query rewriting algorithm is used to push computation to the local endpoints by relying on information about the underlying RDF datasets. It implements a selectivity-aware query execution plan generation.

SPLENDID, CostFed, ANAPSID, SemaGrow, and Odyssey are examples of the hybrid (index+ASK) SPARQL query federation approaches over multiple SPARQL endpoints. SPLENDID performs cost-based optimization using VOID statistics from datasets. It makes use of bind and hash joins [SKH+15]. CostFed also implements a cost-based query planner. The source selection is closely related to HiBISCuS [SNN14]. Both bind and symmetric hash joins are used for data integration. ANAPSID [AVL+11] is an adaptive query federation engine that adapts its query execution at runtime according to the data availability and condition of the SPARQL endpoints. ANAPSID implements adaptive group and adaptive dependent joins [SKH+15]. SemaGrow adapts source selection approach from SPLENDID. It performs a cost-based query planning based on VOID statistics about datasets. SemaGrow implements bind, hash, and merge joins. Odyssey is also a cost-based federation engine. MULDER describes data sources in terms of RDF molecule templates and utilize these template for source selection, and query decomposition and optimization.

DAW [SNNXP+13] and Fedra [MSMMV15] are examples of duplicate-aware query federation approaches over multiple SPARQL endpoints.

SaGe[MSM18] is a stateless preemptable SPARQL query engine for public endpoints. The system makes use of preemptable query plans and time-sharing scheduling, SaGe tackles the problem of RDF data availability for complex queries in public endpoints. Consequently, SaGe provides a convenient alternative to the current practice of copying RDF data dumps.

link traversal based sparql federation: LDQPS [LT10], SI-HJoin [LT11], WoDQA [AHED12], and SQUIN [Har13b] are examples of traversal-based federated SPARQL query processing approaches.

Both LQPS and SIHJoin make use of the index and online discovery via link-traversal to identify the relevant sources pertaining to the given SPARQL query. They implement symmetric hash join. WoDQA performs hybrid (index+ASK) source selection approach. It implements nested loop and bind joins. SQUIN discovers the potentially relevant data during the query execution and thus produce incremental query results. SQUIN uses a heuristic for query execution plan generation, adapted from [Har11]. As a physical implementation of the logical plans, SQUIN uses a synchronized pipeline of iterators such that the i-th operator is responsible for the i-th triple pattern of the given SPARQL query. More recent studies [HÖ16] investigated 14 different approaches to rank traversal steps and achieve a variety of traversal strategies. A more exhaustive survey of the traversal-based SPARQ query federation is provided in [HBF09].

Beside the above query federation strategies, low-cost Triple Pattern Fragments (TPF) interfaces [VVSH⁺16] can also be used to execute federated SPARQL queries. Comunica [TVHVSV18] is a highly modular meta engine for federated SPARQL query evaluation over support heterogeneous interfaces types, including self-descriptive Linked Data interfaces such as TPF. The system also enables querying over heterogeneous sources, such as SPARQL endpoints and data dumps in RDF serializations. The main drawback here is that the user should know in advance the dataset where the query will be executed.

One of the targets and motivation to build WimuQ was to discover which dataset the SPARQL query can be executed, unfortunately, with exception of SQUIN [Har13b], none of the related works provides this feature. Despite the fact that some of them incorporate Nquad support that allows the possibility to know the graph of the triple. The provenance system of WimuQ also includes dump files and endpoints with a rank provided by WIMU [VSN⁺18].

RELATION AMONG LARGE AMOUNT OF RDF SOURCES

In order to find a n a p proach t o r e late a l a rge n u mber o f heterogeneous datasets we start Identifying datasets[VSN+18], then
finding similarities[VSN17b] a n d b u ild a n i n dex o f t h ose similar
datasets[AV20] providing a rank and the provenance.

This chapter is a merge of 3 publications, [VSN+18], [AV20] and [VSN17b], in which are three steps to find relations among a large amount of RDF sources, starting by identifying datasets, then find relationships among those RDF sources using String Similarity.

4.1 IDENTIFYING DATASETS IN LARGE HETEROGENEOUS RDF SOURCES

This part of the book covers the RQ1 and is one of the Semantic Web
foundations, which is the possibility to dereference URIs to let applications negotiate their semantic content. However, this exploitation
is often infeasible as the availability of such information depends on
the reliability of networks, services, and human factors. Moreover,
it has been shown that around 90% of the information published as
Linked Open Data is available as data dumps and more than 60% of
endpoints are offline. T o th is e n d, w e p r opose a W eb s e rvice called
Where is my URI?. Our service aims at indexing URIs and their use
in order to let Linked Data consumers find t h e r e spective R DF data
source, in case such information cannot be retrieved from the URI
alone. We rank the corresponding datasets by following the rationale
upon which a dataset contributes to the definition o f a U RI propor-
tionally to the number of literals. We finally d e scribe p o tential use-
cases of applications that can immediately benefit f r om o u r simple
yet useful service.

4.1.1 *The WIMU approach*

In the Web of Data, applications such as Link Discovery or Data
Integration frameworks need to know where a specific U R I i s lo-
cated. However, due to decentralized architecture of the Web of
data, reliability and availability of Linked Data services, locating such
URIs is not a trivial task. Locating the URIs from a well-known
data dump might be easy. For example, it is trivial to know that
the belongs to the DB-pedia dataset. However, locating the
dataset where was first de-fined is a time-consuming task.
Consequently, this can greatly affect the scalable and time-efficient
deployment of many Semantic Web ap-plications such as link
discovery, Linked Data enrichment, and feder-

ated query processing. On the other hand, such provenance information about URIs can lead to regenerate and validate the links across datasets.

The availability of the current available services to provide such information is unfortunately one of the key issues in Semantic Web and Linked Data. It has been shown that around 90% of the information published as Linked Open Data is available as data dumps only and more than 60% of endpoints are offline [VUM$^+$17]. The availability problem is mostly due to cost associated with storing and providing querying services.

To this end, we propose *Where is my URI?* Where is My URI? (WIMU), a low-cost Semantic Web service to determine the RDF data source of URIs along with their use. We also rank the data sources in case a single URI is provided by multiple data sources. The ranking is based-on a scoring function. Currently, our service processed more than 58 billion unique triples from more than 660,000 datasets obtained from LODStats [ADML12] and LOD Laundromat [BRB$^+$14]. For each URI, our service provides the corresponding datasets and the number of literals in the datasets having this URI. The service is both available from a web interface as well as can be queried from a client application using the standard HTTP protocol. We believe our service can be used in multiple Linked Data related problems such as devising fast link discovery frameworks, efficient source selection, and distributed query processing.

Our main contributions are as follows:

- We provide a regularly updated[1] database index of more than 660K datasets from LODStats and LOD Laundromat.

- We provide an efficient, low cost and scalable service on the web that shows which dataset most likely defines a URI.

- We provide various statistics of datasets indexed from LODStats and LOD Laundromat.

The service is available from under GNU Affero public license 3.0 and the source code is available online[2].

The rest of the chapter is organized as follows: We discuss the proposed approach in detail, including the index creation, the web interface, and the data processing. We finally present our evaluation results.

4.1.2 *The approach*

WIMU uses the number of literals as a heuristic to identify the dataset which most likely defines a U RI. T he i ntuition b ehind t his c an be

---

1 Updated monthly due to the huge size of data processed.
2 Link to the GitHub repository

explained in two points: (1) Literal values are the raw data that can disambiguate a URI node in the most direct way and (2) The Semantic Web architecture expects that datasets reusing a URI only refer to it without defining more literal values. One more reason for point (1) is that: it is straightforward to understand whether two literal values are different, whereas disambiguating URIs usually requires more effort.

We store the collected data in an Apache Lucene[3] index. Due to runtime performance and complexity reasons, we found that storing the information into Lucene was more convenient than a traditional triple store such as Virtuoso[4]. The rationale behind this choice is that a tuple such as *(URI, Dataset, Score)* would be expressed using at least three triples; for instance:

```
:R001 :hasURI :URI001
:R001 :hasDataset :Dataset001
:R001 :hasScore "20"^^
```

where :R001 is an index record URI. Therefore, materializing all records would have substantially increased the space complexity of our index.

The index creation

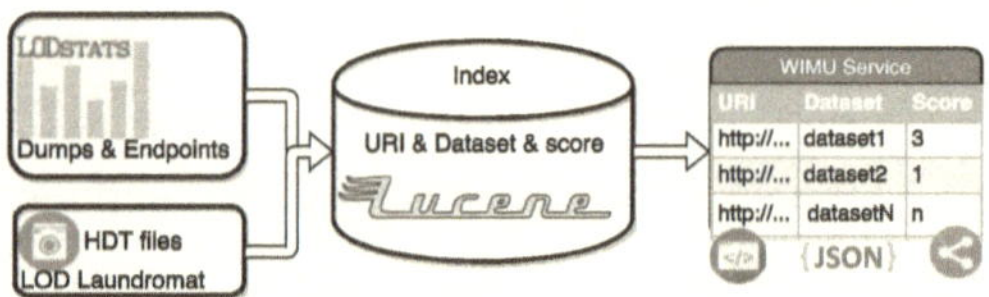

Figure 5: Creation workflow of the WIMU index.

The index creation, the core of our work, is shown in figure 5 and consists in the following four steps:

1. Retrieve list of datasets from sources (i.e., LOD Stats and LOD Laundromat).

2. Retrieve data from datasets (i.e., dump files, endpoints, and HDT files).

3. Build three indexes from dump files, endpoints, and HDT files.

4. Merge the indexes into one.

5. Make the index available and browsable via a web application and an API service.

For each processed dataset, we keep its URI as provenance. After we have downloaded and extracted a dump file, we process it by counting the literals as objects for each subject. For endpoints and HDT files, we use a SPARQL query:

```
SELECT ?s (count(?o) as ?c) WHERE {
    ?s [] ?o . FILTER(isliteral(?o))
} GROUP BY ?s
```

We process the data in parallel, distributing the datasets among the CPUs. If a dataset is too large for a CPU, we split it into smaller chunks. To preserve space, dump files are deleted after being processed. The index was generated using an Intel Xeon Core i7 processor with 64 cores, 128 GB RAM on an Ubuntu 14.04.5 LTS with Java SE Development Kit 8.

The web interface and the API service

In order to simplify the access to our service, we create a web interface where it is possible to visualize all the data from the service, as figure 6 shows.

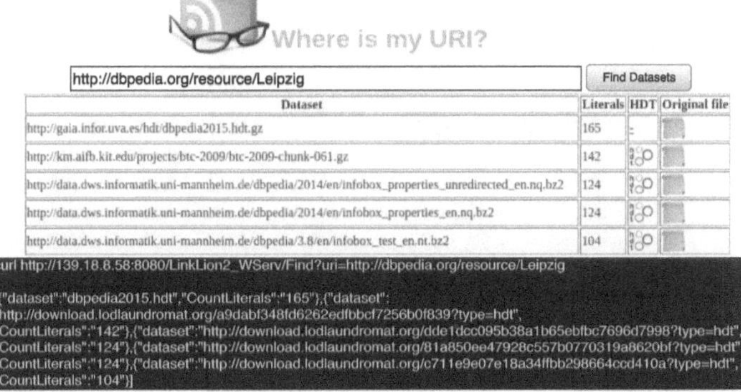

Figure 6: Web interface.

The web interface allows the user to query a URI and see the results in a HTML web browser; the API service allows the user to work with an output in JSON format. In figure 6, we can see an example of usage of the service, where WIMU is requested for the dataset in which the URI dbpedia:Leipzig was defined. figure 8 shows the generic usage of WIMU.

4.1.3   *Use cases*

In this section, we present three use-cases to show that our hypothesis works on the proposed tasks.

Data Quality in Link Repositories

The first use-case is about quality assurance in a link repository by re-applying link discovery algorithms on the stored links. This task concerns important steps of the Linked Data Lifecycle, in particular *Data Interlinking* and *Quality*. Link repositories contain sets of links that connect resources belonging to different datasets. Unfortunately, the subject and the object URIs of a link often do not have meta-data available, hence their Concise Bounded Descriptions (CBDs) are hard to obtain. In following figure, $(D_1, ..., D_n|x) : D_n$ represent the datasets and x is the quantity of literals. The **input** for our service in this use-case is S; the **output** is $\{(D_1, 3), (D_2, 1), (D_3, 2)\}$, where D1 most likely defines S due to the highest number of literal. In the same way, the dataset that most likely defines T is D_4 with 7 literals. Once we have this information, the entire CBD of the two resources S and T can be extracted and a Link Discovery algorithm can check whether the `owl:sameAs` link among them should subsist.

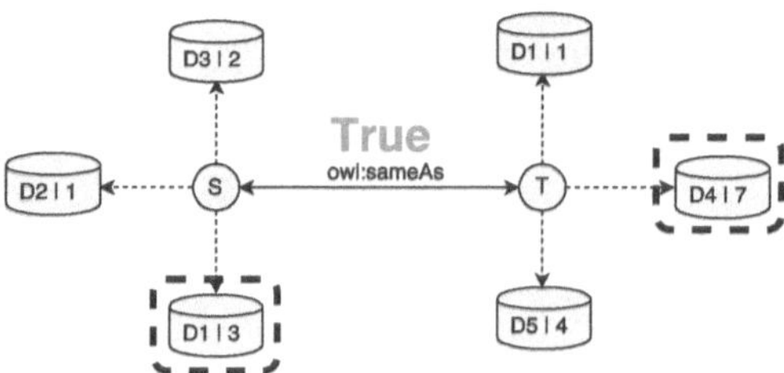

Figure 7: First use-case.

Finding class axioms for Link Discovery

A class axiom is needed by the link discovery algorithm to reduce the number of comparisons. Here, the aim is to find two class axioms for each mapping in the link repository.

To this end, we use real data including a mapping[5] from the LinkLion repository [NSNR14a] between   and   Our service shows that S was defined in four datasets, whereas the dataset with more literals was . Thus, we can deduce where the URI S was most likely defined. Knowing the datasets allows us to extract the axioms of the classes our URIs belong to. The techniques to decrease the complexity vary from choosing the most specific class to using an ontology learning tool such as DL-Learner [Leho9].

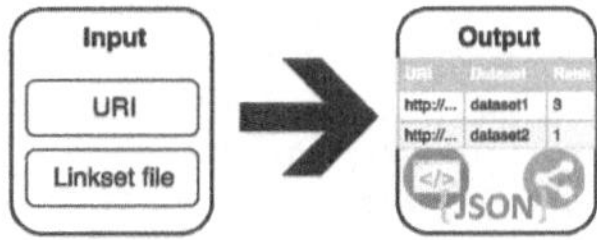

Figure 8: Usage.

Federated Query Processing

Federated queries, which aim to collect information from more than one datasets is of central importance for many semantic web and linked data applications [SKI⁺13; SKI⁺14]. One of the key step in federated query processing is the *source selection*. The goal of the source selection is to find relevant sources (i.e., datasets) for the given user query. In the next step, the federated query processing engine makes use of the source selection information to generate an optimized query execution plan. WIMU can be used by the federated SPARQL engines to find the relevant sources against the individual triple patterns of the given SPARQL query. In particular, our service can be helpful during the source selection and query planning in cost-based SPARQL federation engines such SPLENDID [GS11], SemaGrow [CTK15], HiBISCuS [SNN14], CostFed [PSS⁺17], etc.

Usage examples

The service API provides a JSON as output, allowing users to use WIMU with some programming language compatible with JSON. Here we give examples, for more details please check the manual[7].
  Service: Parameters table 12:
  Input (Single URI example):

  Output:

---

6 Also available in HDT file

7 More examples such as many URIs, linksets, and generation of Concise Bounded Description (CBD)

Table 12: Parameters

Parameter	Default	Description
top	0	Top ocurrences of the datasets where the URI was defined.
uri	-	URI expected to search .

```
{
  "dataset":
  "http://downloads.dbpedia.org/2016-10/core-i18n/en/
      infobox_properties_en.ttl.bz2",
  "CountLiteral": "236"
},
{
  "dataset": "http://gaia.infor.uva.es/hdt/dbpedia2015.hdt.gz",
  "CountLiteral": "165"
},
{
  "dataset":
  "http://download.lodlaundromat.org/
      a9dabf348fd6262edfbbcf7256b0f839?type=hdt",
  "CountLiteral": "142"
},
{
  "dataset":
  "http://download.lodlaundromat.org/
      dde1dcc095b38a1b65ebfbc7696d7998?type=hdt",
  "CountLiteral": "124"
}
]
```

Java and the API Gson[8]:

```java
private void exampleJson() throws Exception {
  String service = "https://wimu.aksw.org/Find?uri=";
  String uri = "http://dbpedia.org/resource/Leipzig";
  URL url = new URL(service + uri);
  InputStreamReader reader = new InputStreamReader(url.openStream());
  WIMUDataset wData = new Gson().fromJson(reader, WIMUDataset[].class)[0];
  System.out.println("Dataset:" + wData.getDataset());
  System.out.println("Dataset(HDT):" + wData.getHdt());
}
```

4.1.4 *Evaluation: Statistics about the Datasets*

To the best of our knowledge, LODStats[ADML12] is the only project oriented to monitoring dump files; however, its last update dates back to 2016. Observing table 13, we are able to say that from LODStats, not all datasets are ready to use. Especially, more than 58% are off-line, 14% are empty datasets, 8% of the triples that have literals as objects are blank nodes and 35% of the online datasets present some error using the Apache Jena parser[9]. A large part of those data was processed and cleaned by LOD Laundromat [BRB+14].

Table 13: Datasets.

	LOD Laundromat	LODStats	Total
URIs indexed	4,185,133,445	31,121,342	4,216,254,787
Datasets checked	658,206	9,960	668,166
Triples processed	19,891,702,202	38,606,408,854	58,498,111,056

The algorithm took three days and seven hours to complete the task. Thus, we will create a scheduled job to update our database index once a month. With respect to the information present in the figure 9, we can observe that the majority of files from LODStats are in RDF/XML format. Moreover, the endpoints are represented in greater numbers (78.6%), the dominant file format is RDF with 84.1% of the cases, and 56.2% of errors occurred because Apache Jena was not able to perform SPARQL queries. Among the HDT files from LOD Laundromat, 2.3% of them could not be processed due to parsing errors. Another relevant point is that 99.2% of the URIs indexed with WIMU come from LOD Laundromat, due to 69.8% of datasets from LODstats contain parser errors in which WIMU was not able to process the data.

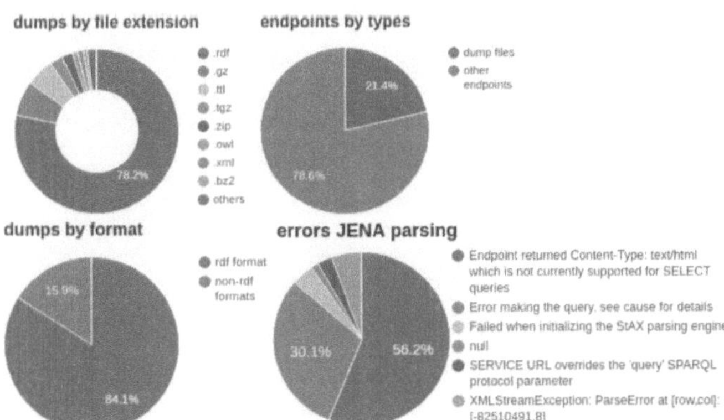

Figure 9: Dump files and Apache Jena parsing error.

Finally, we validated our heuristic assessing if the URI really belongs to the dataset with more literals. To this end, we took a sample of 100 URIs[10] that belong to at least two datasets, where we assess manually the data in order to check if the results are really correct. As a result, the dataset containing the correct information was found

as first result in 90% of the URIs and among the top three in 95% of
the URIs.

4.2 RELATING RDF SOURCES

Here we cover the RQ2, highlighting the challenge where although we have witnessed the growing adoption of Linked Open Data principles for publishing data on the Web, connecting data to third parties remains a difficult and time-consuming task. One question that often arises during the publication process is: "Is there any data set available on the Web we can connect with?". This simple question unfolds a set of others that hinders data publishers to connect to other data sources. For instance, if there are related data sets, where are they? How many? Do they share concepts and properties? How similar are they? Is there any duplicated data set? To answer these questions, this chapter introduces: (i) a new class of data repositories; (ii) a novel method to store and detect data set similarities (duplicated data set and data set chunks); (iii) an index to store data set relatedness; and, (iv) a search engine to find related data sets. To create the index, we harvested more than 668k data sets from LOD Stats and LOD Laundromat, along with 559 active SPARQL endpoints corresponding to 221.7 billion triples or 5 terabytes of data. Our evaluation on state-of-the-art real-data shows that more than 90% of data sets in the LOD Laundromat do not use the *owl:equivalentProperty*, *owl:equivalentClass* nor any other way to relate to one another data, which reaffirms ahd emphasize the importance of our work.

4.2.1 *The ReLOD approach*

People will always describe knowledge in different ways, due to the individuality of the being, different points of view, time and space, in which we assume as a natural phenomenon and standard. Aware of the state of the art from Ontology/Schema/Instance Matching from Linked Data from venues such as Very Large Data Bases (VLDB)[11], Ontology Alignment Evaluation Initiative (OEAI)[12], International Semantic Web Conference (ISWC)[13], European Semantic Web Conference (ESWC)[14], among others, we observe that the LOD datasets are following this standard.

We notice that there are several similar data sets. Yet, there is no place that stores or provides such kind of information about how similar the data sets are and which attributes the data sets share. This work aims to build an index to store the relation among the data sets to have a place to see how similar the data sets are. We provide a method to index the relations among LOD data sets[15] based on the properties and classes that they share.

As a motivation of our work, we describe two distinct scenarios where the proposed index may be useful:

Scenario 1: Given the SPARQL query at Listing 1, where the user wants to know if a given data set contains three properties, in which the user already know the query performs well at the SPARQL endpoint from CKAN[16]:

```
1  SELECT * WHERE { ?s ?p ?o.
2  FILTER(?s=<http://purl.org/dc/terms/date> ||
3  ?s=<http://crime.rkbexplorer.com/id/location> ||
4  ?s=<http://purl.org/dc/terms/subject>
5  )}
```

Listing 1: Scenario 1.

The following questions are raised:

- How to know which data sets are able to execute the query?

- Which of the data sets contains the most valuable results?

- Could the results from different data sets complement each other?

In this case an approach is needed to enable the user to know more datasets to extract the required information. An index of dataset relations/similarities could be used to know that the query can also be executed with results at but not at , and we can execute at least in other five[17] data sets to complement the results.

Scenario 2: The user need information about cities from all datasets in your repository, more specifically datasets that are compatible with the class . Using our previous approach WIMU[VSN⁺18], this URI was found in 11 datasets[18], but how many URIs in other datasets that also represents a city that were not listed, for instance a city at WikiData[19] is represented by . We consider here that to execute such task manually on more than 600,000 datasets is not feasible. Thus, having an index of dataset relation will help in this case.

The contributions of this chapter are:

- A method to create an incremental index of similarity among LOD datasets. Thus, to the best of our knowledge, ReLOD is the first dataset relation index over a net total of 221.7 billion triples.

- A creation of a mechanism to search this index by Dataset URI, property, class or SPARQL query. For the first time, to the best of our knowledge, we make a relation index able to query by dataset URI, property, class or SPARQL query.

- A method to identify duplicated datasets and chunks.

The rest of the chapter is organized as follows: First we present our approach in the Section 6.3 then the Section 4.2.3 shows the evaluation results and discussion.

4.2.2 The approach

Our observations guide us to a method to create an index of LOD datasets, in which involves a compilation of many other works, starting collecting data from more than 650,000 LOD datasets from LODStats, LODLaundromat and more than 500 endpoints[20].

The index creation

Given a set of Datasets $D\{d_1, ..., d_n\}$, assuming d_n represents a RDF dataset[21], in which each d contains a set of properties and classes represented by $\mathcal{P}$. The next step consists in creating a set E containing the identified duplicated datasets. Thus, we can exclude from **D** all datasets contained in **E**.

The goal of algorithm 1[22] is to create an index to store the relations among datasets by comparing the occurrences of classes and properties of each dataset, by String similarity and Instance Matching. The **Input** is a set of Datasets and the **Output** is the index of dataset relations.

figure 10 shows a workflow about how the index is created and the algorithm 1 describe with more details the process of creation of the dataset relation index.

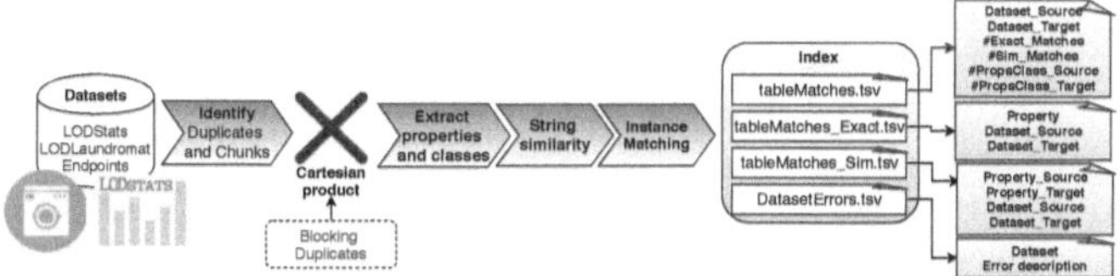

Figure 10: Creating the index.

Figure 11: Querying the index.

Algorithm 1 Creation of the LOD dataset relation index

Input: D, E   ▷ Datasets and datasets duplicated
Output: C, X, Y, Z   ▷ Four tsv files containing the matches(datasets, classes and
properties).
  1: $M_e\{\}$ ▷ HashMap containing datasetTarget and another hash containing
     properties and classes exact matched
  2: $M_s\{\}$ ▷ HashMap containing datasetTarget and another hash containing
     properties and classes matched using String similarity
  3: $M_a\{\}$ ▷ HashMap containing datasets already compared
  4: **D − E**   ▷ Remove duplicates contained in **E**
  5: **T = D**
  6: **for all** d ∈ D **do**   ▷ In parallel
  7:     **for all** t ∈ T **do**
  8:        **if** (d <> t) ∧ **alreadyCompared**(d, t) **then**
  9:           continue   ▷ Skip the current **d** and **t**
10:        **end if**
11:        M_e.add(**getExactMatches**(d, t))   ▷ Add a set containing the
     properties/classes that are exact the same in both datasets
12:        M_s.add(**getSimMatches**(d, t, 0.8, M_e))   ▷ Add a set containing the
     properties that are similar in both datasets, excluding the matches from M_e
13:        M_a.add(d, t)   ▷ Add the dataset pair already processed
14:     **end for**
15: **end for**
16: **printMaps**(M_e, M_s)   ▷ Print the content of M_e and M_s inside the files
    C, X, Y, Z

The function **getExactMatches(d, t))** compares all properties and classes from each dataset **d** and **t** and return a set of properties and classes that are exact the same, keeping the provenance of the dataset.

The function **getSimMatches(d, t,** 0.8, M_e) compares all properties and classes from each dataset **d** and **t** using Jaccard and MFKC[VSN17b] String Similarity function with a threshold of 0.8, excluding the exact matches identified previously by the function **getExactMatches** returning a set of properties and classes that has the similary greater than the threshold 0.8, keeping the provenance of the dataset, the figure 12 shows our string similarity process.

The function **printMaps(M_e, M_s)** print the content from the matching functions into the files according the structure described in section 4.2.2.

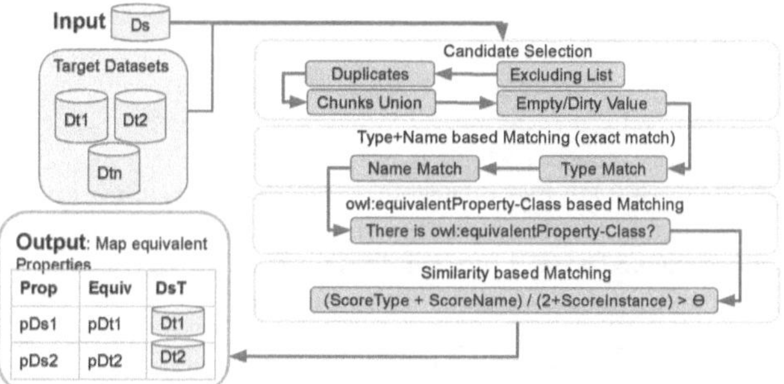

Figure 12: String similarity process.

Identifying duplicated and chunk datasets

With the current hardware available (HD 1Tb, Memory 16GB, processor intel core i7). To compare all LOD datasets, in this case more than 600 thousand datasets, implies in more than 360 billion of comparisons($n * n$), assuming that each comparison takes in average 1 millisecond, the whole operation will take more than 10 years.

Thus, we decided to have a blocking method to avoid unnecessary comparisons. To this aim, we create a way to detect duplicated and chunk-dump-files datasets, described on Algorithmus 2. Our blocking method avoid datasets with less than 1 triple, duplicates, less than 5 properties, less than 5 classes.

The function **eliminateDuplicates()**, identify and eliminate duplicated HDT files by comparing the property occurrences of each dataset and the header metadata.

We formalize the problem of Clustering datasets identifying duplicates and chunks as follows:

We consider a set of K data sources $S_1, ..., S_k$ containing property occurrences $O_1, ..., O_m$. Each of property P is referenced by an URI, e.g., dbo:City[23]. Each S contains a header H, with meta-data about the data in S, such that $H \subset S$.

The goal is to create clusters of datasets C in two groups of elements from K, in which are duplicates D and chunks E, such that $D \subset K : E \subset K : K \subset C$.

We assume that all datasets are not empty and are RDF compatible with the HDT format.

Firstly we create a dense matrix of property occurrence and dataset. Then it was observed a standard in the dense matrix, that for some datasets the occurrence of the properties was exactly the same. Then, we identify that we can put together those datasets to observe more characteristics. In this second phase, we have a sub-collection of our initial collection of datasets and looking into the header metadata of those files we observe that for some files the meta-data is different. Then we have another sub-collection of files with different headers, and manually reading file by file we realize that they are chunks, in other words, part of a bigger dataset.

Thus we have two phases for clustering dataset (1) Put together datasets that present the same occurrence of properties. (2) Read the header metadata and separate files with a different header. The files with different header are chunks and the rest are duplicates[24].

Algorithm 2 Identifying duplicates and chunk

Input: D   ▷ Datasets
Output: **C, X**   ▷ two files chunks.txt and duplicates.txt.

```
 1: sep = t  ▷ Separator for the file, in this case, a tab, but could be another such as
    ";", etc..
 2: setHeader = {}
 3: cSparql = "Select ?p (count(?p) as ?qtd) where ?s ?p ?o . group by ?p"
 4: for all d ∈ D do
 5:     H = getPropertyOccurrence(ds)
 6:     for all key, value ∈ H do ▷ key represent the property and value represents
    the number of occurrences.
 7:         setHeader.add(key)
 8:         line = line + sep + value
 9:     end for
10:     printLineDenseMatrix(d + line)
11:     if setLines.contains(line) then        ▷ Here we identify and put chunks and
    duplicates together
12:         D'.add(d)
13:     else
14:         setLines.add(line)
15:     end if
16: end for
17: printHeaderDenseMatrix(setHeader)
18: C.add(diff(D'))                ▷ Here we separate chunks and duplicates
19: X.add(diffD(D'))
20: return C, X                    ▷ two files chunks.txt and duplicates.txt.
```

The function **getPropertyOccurrence**(ds) returns a hash map containing the property and the number of occurrences of each property from a given dataset with the SPARQL query at Listing 2

```
1  Select ?p (count(?p) as ?qtd) where {?s ?p ?o .} group by ?p
```

Listing 2: Property occurrence query.

The function **printLineDenseMatrix**(line) print a line in a file and the function **printHeaderDenseMatrix**(setHeader) print the first line of the dense matrix file containing the header of the matrix, in which refers to the identification of the properties. The function **diff(D′)** separates the chunks from duplicates, for this task we look into the

---

24 More details, please see the implementation and the documentation on

header of the files, in this case, only HDT files, where duplicates present exactly the same header metadata information and chunks are different respect to the header.

Theorem 1: Let P be a collection of property occurrences of datasets D, such that each D has one P, in which D' represents the cluster candidates, in which are the datasets identified as chunks and duplicates together, and the function **diff()** return the dump-files that are not duplicated. Thus, the output of Algorithm 1 when applied to D, the following hold:

$|\mathbf{diff}(\mathbf{D'})| = 0$

All elements from D' are duplicated datasets.

To identify the chunks:

$|\mathbf{diff}(\mathbf{D'})| > 0$

The result from $\mathbf{diff}(\mathbf{D'})$ are the dump-files identified as chunks.

The file structure

Now we describe the file structure that we created to use our index, which consists of 3 TSV[25] files.

- **tableMatches_Exact.tsv**: Contains the exact match of the properties, with the following fields:
    - **Property**: containing the property URI itself.
    - **Source**: Contains the dataset source where the property was found.
    - **Target**: Contains de dataset matched containing the property.

- **tableMatches_Sim.tsv**: Represents the similarity of properties from datasets Source and Target, with the following fields:
    - **PropertyS**: The property from the dataset Source.
    - **PropertyT**: The property from the dataset Target.
    - **Source**: The dataset Source.
    - **Target**: The dataset Target.

- **tableMatches.tsv**: Represents the datasets Matched and his respectives number of properties exact matched and number of properties matched with String similarity, with the following fields:
    - **Source**: The dataset source.
    - **Target**: The dataset Target.
    - **#ExactMatch**: Number of properties with exact match.
    - **#sim>0.9**: Number of properties with similarity threshold greater than 0.9.

---

25 Tab Separated Value(TSV)

Querying the index

The index provides the following information based on three types of input:

Dataset: The index will provide a list of datasets, number of exact matched[26] properties and number of similar[27] properties.

Set of properties (URIs) separeted by comma:

- Json file containing the property and the list of datasets where this property were found by exact match.
- A table containing the matches by similarity with the following fields:

    Property Source: Representing the property found on the dataset source.

    Property Target: Representing the property found on the dataset target.

    Dataset Source: The name of the dataset source.

    Dataset Target: The name of the dataset target.

SPARQL query: This type of input extracts the set of properties from the SPARQL query and performs the same operation as **Set of properties (URIs) separeted by comma**.

The index is also incremental, allowing to add more datasets to be processed once a month[28]. The prototype is available online for proof of concept online[29] and the figure 11 shows a workflow about how the index is used.

4.2.3 *Evaluation*

This evaluation aims to answer the following questions: (1) How to identify and quantify similar datasets for a given Dataset?[30] (2) How many datasets are most likely to execute a given SPARQL query? (3) How the detection of duplicated and chunk datasets can help in the process of matching a large amount of datasets? (4) How ReLOD increase the number of datasets identified by wimuQ?

The information contained at table 15 and table 16 are used to see how a sample of datasets are similar, we take 8 famous datasets from

---

26 Exact Match where the URI is exact the same following the principle of uniqueness of the URI
27 Similarity match occurs when the similarity of the URI is greater than 0.9 if less we perform Instance matching.
28 Once a month due to the the time to generate that with our hardware takes at least 88 hours
29 Link to the prototype:
30 To know how many datasets are similar to each other.

rdfhdt.org[31] and 12 from [DABO19]. To obtain the results from the table 15. which is to see how similar are the datasets, we use the formula Gleichung (1) and to obtain the results from table 16, to see how much a dataset is contained inside each other we use the formula in the equation 2, where A and B represents datasets source and target. We have an alternative way to visualize this sample data as a graph[32].

$$jaccard(A, B) = \frac{|A \cap B|}{|A \cup B|} \tag{1}$$

$$contained(A, B) = \frac{|A \cap B|}{|A|} \tag{2}$$

To answer the question (1) we give to our approach as input a version of the dataset DBpedia[33], that contains 2339 properties and classes, and as output we can obtain the most similar datasets[34]. Thus we sorted those datasets in a way of Top 10 datasets more similar to DBpedia, according to the properties and classes they share. On the table 17 we show the number of properties that they share that contains the exact same URI and cases where they share not the exact URI but very similar[35]. Thus, an example of application could with a case when the user wants to identify information from other datasets to complement or enrich information for a given dataset, i.e. facilitating federated queries. The table 18 shows a evaluation with 600 randonly chosen datasets[36] including 3 synthetic manually made datasets.

With our experiments we realize that more than 50% of properties and classes has a match in another dataset. The information can also be observed at figure 13(a), with 600 datasets from LODLaundromat[BRB+14], in which highlight the high possibility that one dataset can enrich each other with complementing information from another dataset.

The time consumed can be observed on figure 13(b), with 600 datasets from LODLaundromat[BRB+14], which shows that 100 million triples were processed in less than 8 minutes, in which is a acceptable time, in which the starts to be time-consuming only after 1 million triples.

As we are using WimuQ[VSS19] to identify datasets for a given SPARQL query together with our matching algorithm, we can answer the question (2) based on famous Sparql queries from two real-data federated SPARQL querying benchmarks *LargeRDF-Bench* [SHN16],*FedBench* [SGH+11] and one non-federated real data

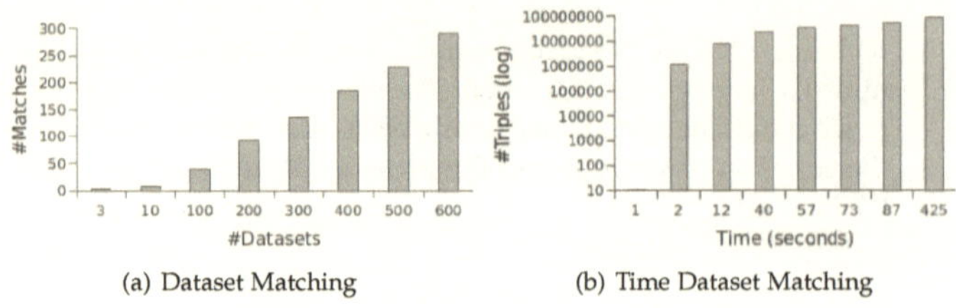

(a) Dataset Matching   (b) Time Dataset Matching

Figure 13: Dataset matching.

SPARQL benchmark selected from *FEASIBLE* [SMN15]. Thus, from the selected datasets we use our approach to select the datasets according to the properties and classes they share among them[37].

To answer the question (3) we evaluate the dataset duplicated detection algorithm and the detection of dataset chunks. From a 5446 datasets[38] our algorithm detected 2272 duplicates and 1470 chunks in 3 hours.

The figure 14(a) shows a case with 900 datasets chosen randomly, where we identified in 10 cases in which we can see the difference

The figure 14(b) show how many chunks we were able to identify among our sample data, in which lead us to know how segregated is data analysed, giving also the chance to know the complete dataset after the union of all chunks.

The current version of the index prototype has information about 539 SPARQL endpoints from LOD cloud[39] and 915 HDT files from LOD Laundromat. We perform more than 1800000 comparisons in 88 hours.

Where **DsPropMatch** on the table 18 refers to the number of properties/classes the datasets share among each other.

We can observe the quantity of properties/classes that the datasets share related to the number of triples analysed. For instance, from 600 datasets, 291 matches where found, in which the number of triples was almost the double size of the previous case. Thus, the number of matches in this case cannot be directly related to the number of triples. Due to this fact, the quality of the datasets should be considerate a important phase.

We evaluate the accuracy of our matching algorithm with a small sample, where we can see at figure 14(c), 14 and 14(d) the F-Measure and run-time on six famous pairs of datasets from[GON18], with those datasets we create a gold standard to compare, in which $P_1...P_n$

---

37 In this case, all datasets identified by wimuQ are sharing properties and classes, that is why we are using the graph from [VSS19].
38 A subset from those 600 datasets chosen previously
39 The list of is available here:

represents the pair of datasets and P1, P2 are datasets synthetically generated by the author, i.e. P3 represents the comparison between the datasets Abt and Buy.

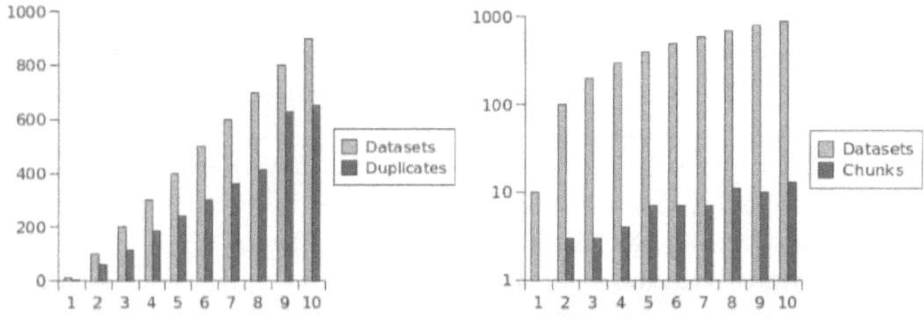

(a) Duplicates identified in 900 datasets. Y axis represents the number of datasets

(b) Chunks identified in 900 datasets. Y axis represents the number of datasets

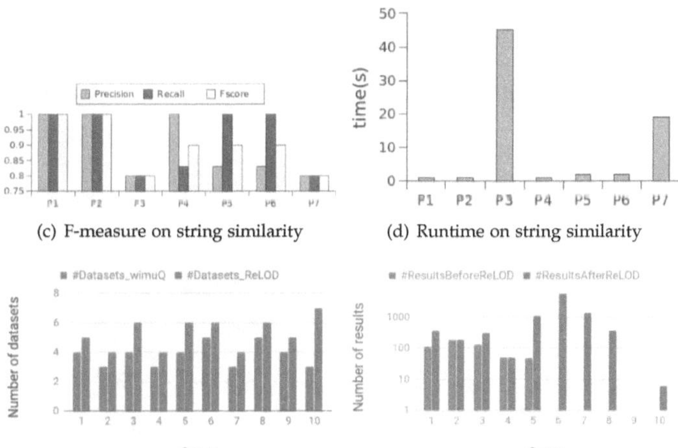

(c) F-measure on string similarity

(d) Runtime on string similarity

(e) Number of datasets identified by wimuQ using ReLOD

(f) Number of results identified by wimuQ using ReLOD. (Vertical axis in log scale)

Figure 14: Improvements of ReLOD.

The figure 9 shows that the majority of files from LODStats are in RDF/XML format. Moreover, the endpoints are represented in greater numbers (78.6%), the dominant file format is RDF with 84.1% of the cases, and 56.2% of errors occurred because Apache Jena was not able to perform SPARQL queries. Among the HDT files from LOD Laundromat, 2.3% of them could not be processed due to parsing errors. Another relevant point is that 99.2% of the URIs indexed with WIMU come from LOD Laundromat, due to 69.8% of datasets from LODstats contain parser errors in which WIMU was not able to process the data.

To answer the question (4) we selected 10 queries[40] from FedBench[SGH+11], where we can observe on the figure 14(e) that thanks to the ReLOD approach we could increase the number of datasets identified by wimuQ, i.e., in query 5, using ReLOD allowed us to find 2 more datasets containing complementary information.

On the other hand, the figure 14(f) reinforces that more datasets do not always imply in more results, i.e., in query 2 and 4, more datasets were identified, but the number of results did not change, in this case, the reason was that the datasets identified by ReLOD were practically the same with different property and class names. The results from queries 6 to 10 were only found thanks to the ReLOD approach[41].

4.3 RELATING SIMILAR RESOURCES USING STRING SIMILARITY

To relate the datasets it is necessary to identify links among them. In this chapter, we cover the RQ3 discussing how linking entries across heterogeneous data sources such as databases or knowledge bases, which becomes an increasingly difficult problem, in particular w.r.t. the runtime of these tasks. Consequently, it is of utmost importance to provide time-efficient approaches for similarity joins in the Web of Data. While a number of scalable approaches have been developed for various measures, the Most Frequent k Characters (MFKC) measure has not been tackled in previous works. We hence present a sequence of filters that allow discarding comparisons when executing bounded similarity computations without losing recall. Therewith, we can reduce the runtime of bounded similarity computations by approximately 70%. Our experiments with a single-threaded, a parallel and a GPU implementation of our filters suggest that our approach scales well even when dealing with millions of potential comparisons.

4.3.1 *The MFKC approach*

The problem of managing heterogeneity at both the semantic and syntactic levels among various information resources [VAK15; SE13] is one of the most difficult problems on the information age. This is substantiated by most of the database research self-assessment reports, which acknowledge that the hard question of semantic heterogeneity, that is of handling variations in meaning or ambiguity in entity interpretation, remains open [SE13]. In knowledge bases, Ontology Matching (OM) solutions address the semantic heterogeneity problem in two steps: (1) matching entities to determine an alignment, i.e., a set of correspondences, and (2) interpreting an alignment according to application needs, such as data translation or query answering. Record Linkage (RL) and, more recently, Link Discovery[42] (LD) solutions on the other hand aim to determine pairs of entries that abide by a given relation R. In both cases, string similarities are used to compute candidates for alignments. In addition to being central to RL and LD, these similarities also play a key role in several other tasks such as data translation, ontology merging and navigation on the Web of Data [SE13; ES⁺07].

One of the core tasks when developing time-efficient RL and LD solutions hence lies in the development of time-efficient string similarities. In this paper, we study the MFKC similarity function [SAAM14] and present an approach for improving the performance of similarity joins. To this end, we develop a series of filters which guarantee that

---

42 The expression "link discovery" in this paper means the discovery of typed relations that link instances from knowledge bases on the Web of Data. We never use it in the sense of graph theory.

particular pairs of resources do not abide by their respective similarity threshold by virtue of their properties.

The contributions of this paper are as follows:

1. We present two nested filters, (1) First Frequency Filter and (2) Hash Intersection filter, that allow to discard candidates before calculating the actual similarity value, thus giving a considerable performance gain.

2. We present the k *similarity filter* that allows detecting whether two strings s and t are similar in a fewer number of steps.

3. We evaluate our approach with respect to its runtime and its scalability with several threshold settings and dataset sizes.

4. We present several parallel implementations of our approach and show that they work well on problems where $|D_s \times D_t| \geqslant 10^5$ pairs.

The rest of the chapter is structured as follows: In section 4.3.2, we present our nested filters that allow reducing the runtime of the MFKC similarity joins. We then evaluate our approach in section 4.3.4, where we focus on approaches that aim to improve the time-efficiency of the link discovery task.

4.3.2 *Approach*

Let us call NaiveMFKC the function which computes the MFKC algorithm as described in [SAAM14]. Such function works with three parameters, i.e. two strings s and t and an integer lim and returns the sum of frequencies, where $f(c_i, s)$ is a function that returns the frequency of the character c_i in the string s and $s \supseteq \{c_1, ..., c_n\}$, i.e $f(a, "andrea") = 2$, because the character a has been found twice and the hash functions $h(s)$ and $h(t)$ containing the characters and their frequencies. The output of function is always positive, as shown in equation 3.

$$NaiveMFKC(s, t, lim) = lim - \sum_{c_i \in h(s) \cap h(t)}^{2} f(c_i, s) + f(c_i, t) \qquad (3)$$

Our work aims to reduce the runtime of computation of the MFKC similarity function. Here, we use a sequence of filters, which allow discarding similarity computations and imply in a reduction of runtime. As input, the algorithm receives datasets D_s and D_t, an integer number representing the k most frequent characters and a threshold $\theta \in [0, 1]$. The similarity score of the pair of strings from the Cartesian product from D_s and D_t must have a score greater or equal the threshold θ to be considered a good pair, i.e. for a given threshold θ, if the similarity function has a pair of strings with similarity score less than the threshold, $\sigma(s,t) < \theta$, we can discard the computation of the MFKC score for this pair. Our final result is a set which contains the pairs having similarity score greater than or equal to the threshold, i.e. $\sigma(s,t) \geqslant \theta$.

Our work studies the following problem: Given a threshold $\theta \in [0,1]$ and two sets of strings D_s and D_t, compute the set $M' = \{(s,t,\sigma(s,t)) \in D_s \times D_t \times \mathbb{R}^+ : \sigma(s,t) \geqslant \theta\}$. Two categories of approaches can be considered to improve the runtime of measures: Lossy approaches return a subset M'' of M' which can be calculated efficiently but for which there are no guarantees that $M'' = M'$. Lossless approaches, on the other hand, ensure that their result set M'' is exactly the same as M'. In this paper, we present a lossless approach that targets the MFKC algorithm. Equation 4 shows our definition for the string similarity function σ for the MFKC.

$$\sigma(s,t) = \frac{\sum_{c_i \in h(s,k) \cap h(t,k)} f(c_i,s) + f(c_i,t)}{|s| + |t|} \qquad (4)$$

where s and t are strings, such that $s,t \in \sum^*$, $f(c_i,s)$ is a function that returns the frequency of the character c_i in the string s, where $s \supseteq \{c_1, ..., c_n\}$, k represents the limitation of the elements that belongs to the hashes; set $h(s,k) \cap h(t,k)$ means the intersection between the keys of hashes $h(s,k)$ and $h(t,k)$ (i.e., the most frequent K characters). We expect two steps to obtain the similarity score:

1. Firstly, we transform the strings s and t in two hashes using Most Frequent Character Hashing [SAAM14], according to the following example with $k = 3$:

   $s = aabbbcc \rightarrow h(s,k) = \{b = 3, a = 2, c = 2\}$
   $t = bbccddee \rightarrow h(t,k) = \{b = 2, c = 2, d = 2\}$

2. We calculate the sum of the character frequencies of matching characters on the hashes $h(s,k)$ and $h(t,k)$, then, we normalize dividing by the sum of the length of $|s|$ and $|t|$ resulting in a similarity score from 0 to 1 according to the equation 5 and the resulting score should be greater or equals the threshold θ.

$$\sigma(s,t,k,\theta) = \frac{\sum_{c_i \in h(s,k) \cap h(t,k)} f(c_i,s) + f(c_i,t)}{|s| + |t|} \geqslant \theta \qquad (5)$$

Improving the Runtime

In this section, the runtime of MFKC defined in equation 4 is improved using filters where $\mathcal{N}$ is the output of first frequency filter, $\mathcal{L}$ is the output of hash intersection filter and $\mathcal{A}$ represents the output of the k similarity filter.

First Frequency Filter

As specified in the definition of MFKC [SAAM14] this filter assumes that the hashes are already sorted in an descending way according to the frequencies of characters, therefore the first element of each hash has the highest frequency.

Theorem 1. *Showing that:*

$$\sigma(s,t) = \frac{\sum_{c_i \in h(s,k) \cap h(t,k)} f(c_i, s) + f(c_i, t)}{|s| + |t|} \leqslant \frac{h_1(s,k)k + |t|}{|s| + |t|} \tag{6}$$

implies that $\sigma(s,t) < \theta$.

Theorem 1. Let the intersection between hashes $h(t,k)$ and $h(s,k)$ be a set of characters from c_1 to c_n, such that equation 7:

$$h(t,k) \cap h(s,k) = \{c_1, ..., c_n\} \tag{7}$$

According to the definition of the frequencies $f(()c_i, t)$ we have equation 8:

$$t \supseteq \{c_1, ..., c_1, ..., c_n, ...c_n\} \tag{8}$$

where each c_i appears $f(()c_i, t)$ times, therefore:

$$f(()c_1, t) + ... + f(()c_n, t) \leqslant |t| \tag{9}$$

Also, as $n \leqslant k$, because $t \supseteq \{c_1, ..., c_n\}$, and $f(()c_i, s) \leqslant h_1(s,k) \ \forall_{i=1,...,n}$, then:

$$f(()c_1, s) + ... + f(()c_n, s) \leqslant h_1(s,k) + ... + h_1(s,k) = n(k) \leqslant k(h_1(s,k)) \tag{10}$$

Therefore, from equation 9 and equation 10, we obtain the equation 11:

$$\frac{\sum_{c_i \in h(s,k) \cap h(t,k)} f(c_i, s) + f(c_i, t)}{|s| + |t|} = \frac{\sum_{i=1}^{n} f(()c_i, t) + \sum_{i=1}^{n} f(()c_i, s)}{|s| + |t|}$$
$$\leqslant \frac{h_1(s,k)k + |t|}{|s| + |t|} \tag{11}$$

Consequently, the rule which the filter relies on is the following.

$$\langle s,t \rangle \notin \mathcal{N} \Rightarrow \langle s,t \rangle \notin D_s \times D_t \wedge \frac{h_1(s,k)k + |t|}{|s| + |t|} \leqslant \theta \tag{12}$$

$\square$

Hash Intersection Filter

In this filter, we check if the intersection between two hashes is an empty set, then the MFKC, represented by σ, will return a similarity score of 0 and we can avoid the computation of similarity in this case. Consequently, the rule which the filter relies on is the following.

$$\langle s, t \rangle \in \mathcal{L} \Rightarrow \langle s, t \rangle \in D_s \times D_t \wedge |h(s) \cap h(t)| > 0 \tag{13}$$

we also can say that the equation 14 represents a valid implication.

$$h(s) \cap h(t) = \emptyset \Rightarrow \sigma(s, t) = 0 \tag{14}$$

The equation 14 means that if the intersection between $h(s, k)$ and $h(t, k)$ is a empty set, this implies that the similarity score will be 0. That means there is no character matching, then there is no need to compute the similarity for this pair of strings.

K Similarity filter

For all the pairs left, the similarity score among them is calculated. After that, the third filter selects the pairs whose similarity score is greater or equal than a threshold θ.

$$\langle s, t \rangle \in \mathcal{A} \Leftrightarrow \langle s, t \rangle \in \mathcal{N} \wedge \sigma(s, t) \geq \theta \tag{15}$$

This filter provides a validation and we show that the score of previous k similarity is always lower than the next k, according to the equation 16 and in some cases when the similarity score is been reached before compute all elements $\in h(s, k) \cap h(t, k)$, thus saving computation in these cases.

Here k is also used as a index of similarity function $\sigma_k(s, t)$ in order to get the similarity of all cases of k, from 1 to k, also to show the monotonicity.

Therefore we can say that the computation of similarity score occurs until $\sigma_k(s, t) \geq \theta$.

We will demonstrate that the similarity score of previous k similarity is always lower than the next k similarity, for all $k \in \mathbb{Z}^* : k \leq |s \cap t|$.

$$\sigma_{k+1}(s, t) \geq \sigma_k(s, t) \tag{16}$$

We rewrote the equation for the first iteration, according to equation 17

$$\sigma_k(s, t) = \frac{\sum_{c_i \in h(s,k) \cap h(t,k), i=1}^{k} f(c_i, s) + f(c_i, t)}{|s| + |t|} \tag{17}$$

Let $k \in \mathbb{Z}_+$ be given and suppose the equation 16 is true for $k+1$.

$$\sum_{c_i \in h(s,k) \cap h(t,k)} \left[f(c_i, s) + f(c_i, t) \right] + f(c_{k+1}, s) + f(c_{k+1}, t)$$

$$\geqslant \sum_{c_i \in h(s,k) \cap h(t,k)} f(c_i, s) + f(c_i, t) \tag{18}$$

Therefore, we can notice that the sum of frequencies will be always greater or equal 0, according to $f(c_{k+1}, s) + f(c_{k+1}, t) \geqslant 0$. Thus, equation 16 holds true.

Filter sequence

The sequence of the filters occurs basically in 4 steps, (1) We starting to make the Cartesian product with the pairs of strings from the datasets D_s and D_t, (2) Discarding pairs using the First Frequency Filter($\mathcal{N}$), (3) Discarding pairs where there is no matching characters with the Hash Intersection filter($\mathcal{L}$) and (4) With the Most Frequent Character Filter ($\mathcal{A}$) we will process only similarities greater or equal the threshold θ, if the similarity function $\sigma(s, t) \geqslant \theta$ in the first k characters we can stop the computation of the similarity of this pair, saving computation and add to our dataset with resulting pairs Dr, also shown in the algorithm 3.

4.3.3 *Correctness and Completeness*

In this section, we prove formally that our MFKC is both correct and complete.

- We say that an approach is correct if the output O it returns is such that $O \subseteq R(D_s, D_t, \sigma, \theta)$.

- Approaches are said to be complete if their output O is a superset of $R(D_s, D_t, \sigma, \theta)$, i.e., $O \supseteq R(D_s, D_t, \sigma, \theta)$.

Our MFKC consists of three nested filters, each of which creates a subset of pairs, i.e. $\mathcal{A} \subseteq \mathcal{L} \subseteq \mathcal{N} \subseteq D_s \times D_t$. For the purpose of clearness, we name each filtering rule:

$$R_1 \triangleq \frac{h_1(s,k)k + |t|}{|s| + |t|} < \theta$$

$$R_2 \triangleq |h(s,k) \cap h(t,k)| \neq 0$$

$$R_3 \triangleq \sigma(s,t) \geqslant \theta$$

Each subset of our MFKC can be redefined as $\mathcal{N} = \{\langle s,t \rangle \notin D_s \times D_t : R_1, \mathcal{L} = \{\langle s,t \rangle \in D_s \times D_t : R_1 \wedge R_2, \text{ and } \mathcal{A} = \{\langle s,t \rangle \in D_s \times$

Algorithm 3 MFKC Similarity Joins

1: $GoodPairs = \{s_1; t_1, ..., s_n; t_n\} | \langle s, t \in \sum^* \rangle$
2: $hs = \{e_1, e_2, ..., e_n\} | e_i = \langle c, f(c, s) \rangle$
3: $ht = \{e_1, e_2, ..., e_n\} | e_i = \langle c, f(c, t) \rangle$
4: $i, freq \in \mathbb{N}^*$
5: **procedure** $\mathrm{MFKC}(D_s, D_t, \theta, k)$
6:     **for all** $s \in D_s$ **do (in parallel)**
7:         $hs = h(s, k)$
8:         **for all** $t \in D_t$ **do (in parallel)**
9:            $ht = h(t, k)$
10:            **if** $\frac{hs_1(k) + |t|}{|s| + |t|} < \theta$ **then**
11:              $Next\ t \in D_t$
12:            **end if**
13:            **if** $|hs \cap ht| = 0$ **then**
14:              $Next\ t \in D_t$
15:            **end if**
16:            **for all** $c_{freq} \in hs \cap ht$ **do**
17:              **if** $i \geq k$ **then**
18:                $Next\ t \in D_t$
19:              **end if**
20:              $freq = freq + c_{freq}$
21:              $\sigma_i = \frac{freq}{|s| + |t|}$
22:              **if** $\sigma_i \geq \theta$ **then**
23:                $GoodPairs.add(s, t)$
24:                $Next\ t \in D_t$
25:              **end if**
26:              $i = i + 1$
27:            **end for**
28:         **end for**
29:     **end for**
30:     **return** $GoodPairs$
31: **end procedure**

$D_t : R_1 \wedge R_2 \wedge R_3$. We then introduce $\mathcal{A}^*$ as the set of pairs whose similarity score is more or equal than the threshold θ.

$$\mathcal{A}^* = \{\langle s, t \rangle \in D_s \times D_t : \sigma(s, t) \geqslant \theta\} = \{\langle s, t \rangle \in D_s \times D_t : R_3\} \quad (19)$$

Theorem 2. *Our MFKC filtering algorithm is correct and complete.*

Theorem 2. Proving theorem 2 is equivalent to showing that $\mathcal{A} = \mathcal{A}^*$. Let us consider all the pairs in $\mathcal{A}$. While our MFKC's correctness follows directly from the definition of $\mathcal{A}$, it is complete iff none of pairs discarded by the filters actually belongs to $\mathcal{A}^*$. Assuming that the hashes are sorted in a descending way according the frequencies of the characters, therefore the first element of each hash has the highest frequency. Therefore, once we have

$$\frac{h_1(s,k)k + |t|}{|s| + |t|} < \theta,$$

the pair of strings s and t can be discarded without calculating the entire similarity. When rule R_3 applies, we have $\sigma(s,t) < \theta$, which leads to $R_3 \Rightarrow R_1$. Thus, set $\mathcal{A}$ can be rewritten as:

$$\mathcal{A} = \{\langle s,t \rangle \in D_s \times D_t : R_2 \wedge R_3\} \tag{20}$$

We are given two strings s and t and the respective hashes $h(s,k)$ and $h(t,k)$, the intersection between the characters of these two hashes is a empty set. Therefore, there is no character matching, which implies that s and t cannot be considered to have a similarity score greater than or equal to threshold θ:

$$h(s,k) \cap h(t,k) = \emptyset \Rightarrow \sigma(s,t) = 0$$

When the rule R_3 applies, we have $\sigma(s,t) < \theta$, which leads to $R_3 \Rightarrow R_2$. Thus, set $\mathcal{A}$ can be rewritten as:

$$\mathcal{A} = \{\langle s,t \rangle \in D_s \times D_t : R_3\} \tag{21}$$

which is the definition of $\mathcal{A}^*$ in equation 19. Therefore, $\mathcal{A} = \mathcal{A}^*$.   □

Time complexity

In order to calculate the time complexity of our MFKC, firstly we considered the most frequent K characters from a string. The first step is to sort the string lexically. Then, we can reach a linear complexity after this sort, because the input with highest occurrences can be achieved with a linear time complexity. The first string can be sorted in $O(n\log n)$ and second string in $O(m\log m)$ times, as some classical sorting algorithms such as merge sort [GvN48] and quick sort [Hoa62] that work in $O(n\log n)$ complexity. Thus, the total complexity is $O(n\log n) + O(m\log m)$, resulting in $O(n\log n)$ as upper bound in the worst case.

4.3.4 Evaluation

The aim of our evaluation is to show that our work outperforms the naive approach and the parallel implementation has a performance gain in large datasets with size greater than 10^5 pairs. A considerable number of pairs reach the threshold θ before reaching the last k most frequent character, that also is a demonstration about how much computation was avoided. Instead of all k's we just need $k - n$ where n is the nth most frequent character necessary to reach the threshold θ. An example to show the efficiency of each filter can be found at figure 15, where 10,273,950 comparisons from DBpedia+LinkedGeoData were performed and Performance Gain $(PG) = Recall(\mathcal{N}) + Recall(\mathcal{L})$. The recall can be seen in figure 16(c). This evaluation has the intention to show results of experiments on data from DBpedia[43] and LinkedGeoData[44]. We considered pairs of labels in order to do the evaluation. We have two motivations to chose these datasets: (1) they have been widely used in experiments pertaining to Link Discovery (2) the distributions of string sizes between these datasets are significantly different [DN14]. All runtime and scalability experiments were performed on a Intel Core i7 machine with 8GB RAM, a video card NVIDIA NVS4200 and running Ms Windows 10.

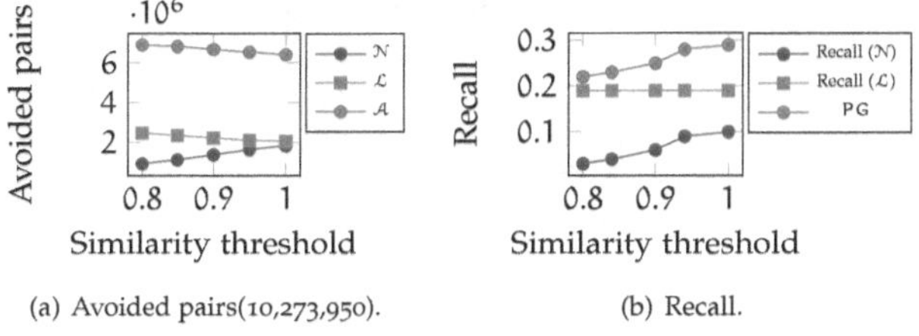

(a) Avoided pairs(10,273,950).   (b) Recall.

Figure 15: Avoided pairs and recall.

Parallel implementation

Our algorithm contains parallel code snippets with which we perform a load and balance of the data among CPU/GPU cores when available. To illustrate this part of our idea, we can state: Given a two datasets S, T, that contains all the strings to be compared. Thus, make a Cartesian product of the strings $S \times T$, where each pair is the processed separately in threads that are spread among CPU/GPU cores. Thus, we process the each comparison in parallel. The parallel implementation works better in large datasets with size more than 10^5, that was more than one time faster than the approach without parallelism and two times faster than the naive approach as shown in figures 17(a), 17(b) and 17(c).

Runtime Evaluation

The evaluation in figures 17(a) and 17(b) shows that all filter setup outperform the naive approach, and the parallel approach does not suffer significant changes related to the runtime according to the size of the dataset, as show figure 17(c). The experiments related to the variance of k, also were considered, as show in figure 18(a), the run-time varies according the size of k, indicating the influence of k with values from 1 to 120 with $1,001,642$ comparisons. The performance (run-time) was improved as shown in figures 17(a), 17(b) and according the recall with a performance gain of 26.07% as shown in figure 15. The time complexity is based on two sort process O(n log n) + O(m log m) resulting in O(n log n) as a upper bound in the worst case.

Scalability Evaluation

In the experiments (see figures 17(c), 18(b) and 18(c)), we looked at the growth of the runtime of our approach on datasets of growing sizes. The results show that the combination of filters $(\mathcal{N} + \mathcal{L} + \mathcal{A})$ is the best option for datasets of large sizes. This result holds on both DBpedia and LinkedGeoData, so our approach can be used on large datasets and achieves acceptable run-times. We also can realize the quantity of avoided pairs in each combination of filters in figure 15, that consequently brings a performance gain. We looked at experiments with runtime behavior on a large dataset with more than 10^6 labels as shown in figure 17(b). The results suggest that the runtime decreases according to the threshold θ increment. Thus, one more point showing that our approach is useful on large datasets, where can be used with high threshold values for link discovery area. About our parallel implementation, figure 17(c) shows that our GPU parallel implementation works better on large datasets with size greater than 10^5.

Comparison with existing approaches

Our work overcomes the naive approach [SAAM14], thus, in order to show some important points we compare our work not only with the state of the art, but with popular algorithms such as Jaccard Index [Jac12]. As shown in figures 17(c), 18(b) and 18(c), our approach outperforms not only the naive approach, but also Jaccard Index. We show that the threshold θ and k have a significant influence related to the runtime. The naive approach present some points to consider, among them, even if the naive approach states that they did experiments with k=7, the naive algorithm was designed for only k=2, there are some cases where $k = 2$ is not enough to get the similarity level expected, i.e. $s = \text{mystring1}$ and $t = \text{mystring2}$ limiting $k = 2$, we will have $\sigma_2(s,t) = 0.2$, showing that the similarity is very low, but when $k = 8$, the similarity is $\sigma_8(s,t) = 0.8$ showing that sometimes we can lose a good similarity case limiting $k = 2$. Our work fix all these problems and also has a better runtime, as show figure 17(a), figure 17(b) and figure 17(c).

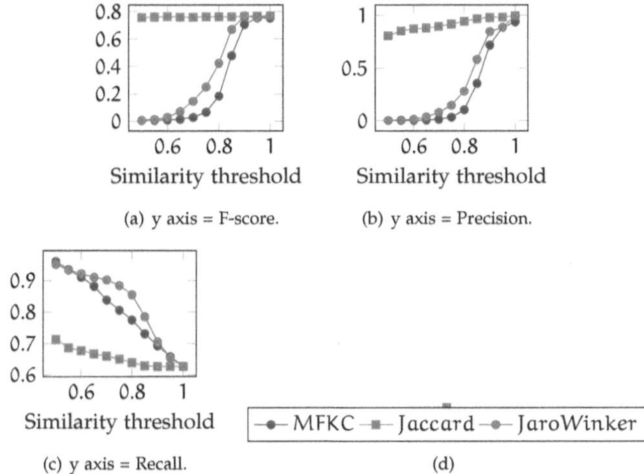

(a) y axis = F-score.   (b) y axis = Precision.

(c) y axis = Recall.   (d)

Figure 16: Precision, Recall and F-Measure.

An experiment with labels from DBpedia and Yago[45] shows that the f-score indicates a significant potential to be used with success as a string similarity comparing with Jaccard Index and Jaro Winkler, as figures 16(a), 16(b) and 16(c) shows. To summarize the key features that makes our approach outperform the naive approach are the following: We use more than two K most frequent characters in our evaluation, our run-time for more than 10^7 comparisons is shorter (27,594 against 16,916) milliseconds, we do have a similarity threshold, allowing us to discard comparisons avoiding extra processing, and a parallel implementation, making our approach scalable. Jaccard does not show significant changes varying the threshold, MFKC and Jaro Winkler present a very similar increase of the f-score varying the threshold.

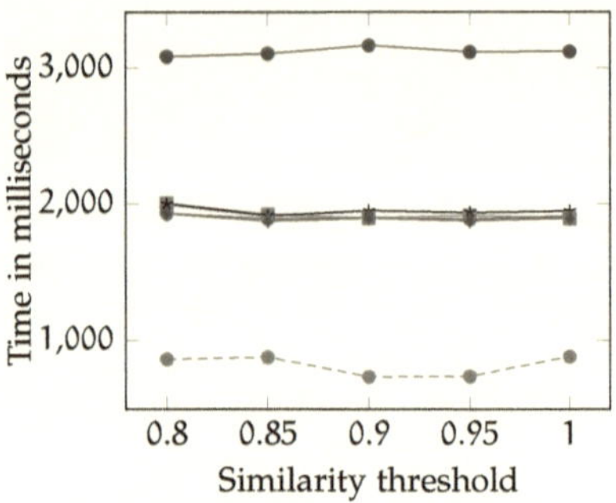

(a) Runtime 1,001,642 comparisons.

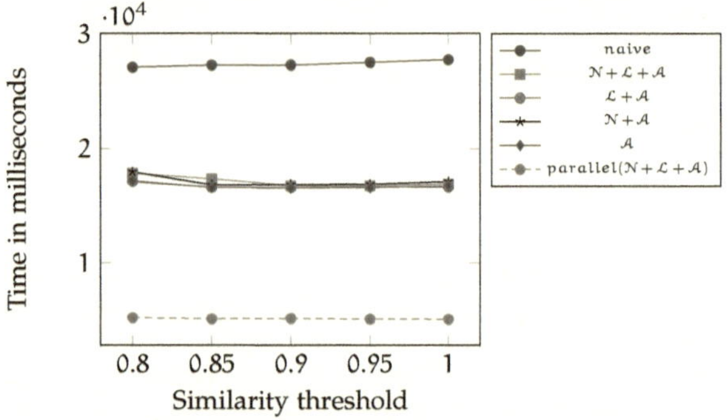

(b) Runtime 10,273,950 comparisons.

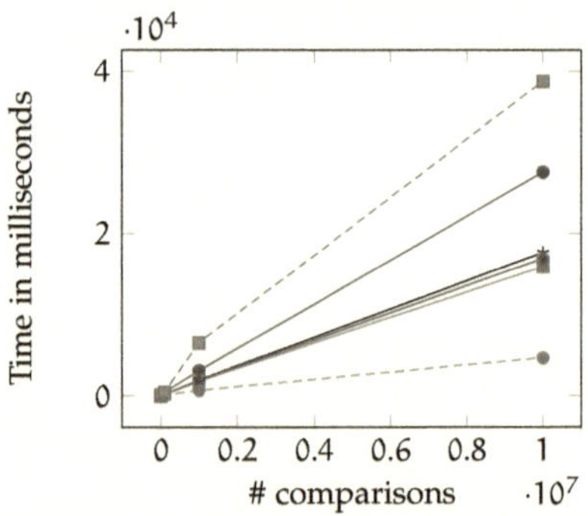

(c) The parallel approach improves the performance for more than 10^5 comparisons.

Figure 17: Run-time experiments results.

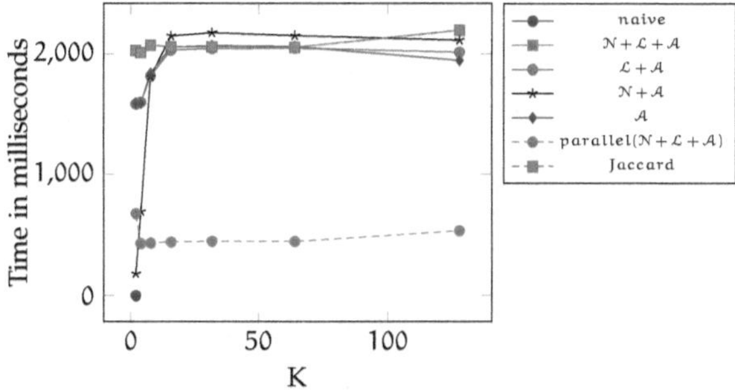

(a) Runtime k most frequent characters, with values of k from 1 to 120, over $1,001,642$ comparisons, $\theta = 0.95$.

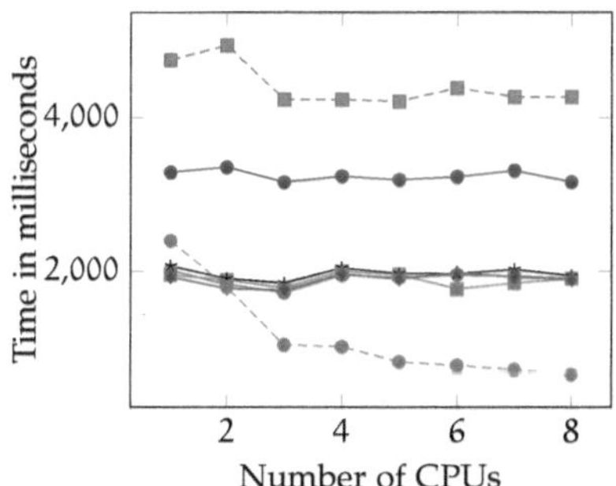

(b) CPU Speedup of algorithm ($1,001,642$ comparisons).

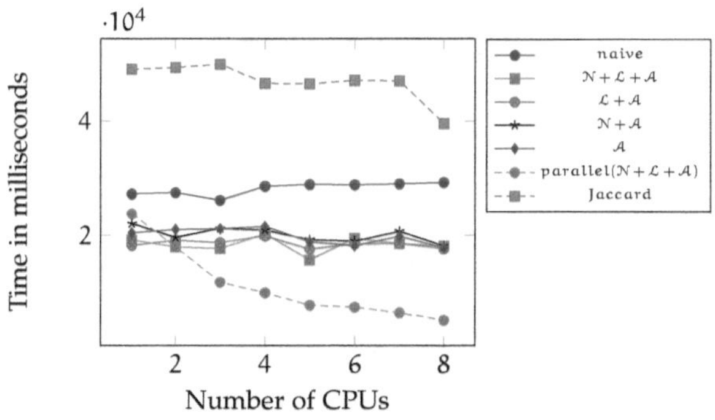

(c) CPU Speedup of algorithm ($10,273,950$ comparisons).

Figure 18: Run-time experiments results.

Table 14: Sample datasets from [GON18] to evaluate our string similarity approach.

Data set	Source (S)	Target (T)	$|S| \times |T|$	Source Property	Target Property
(P3)Abt-Buy	Abt	Buy	1.20×10^6	product name, description manufacturer, price	product name, description manufacturer, price
(P4)Amazon-GP	Amazon	Google Products	4.40×10^6	product name, description manufacturer, price	product name, description manufacturer, price
(P5)DBLP-ACM	ACM	DBLP	6.00×10^6	title, authors venue, year	title, authors venue, year
(P6)DBLP-Scholar	DBLP	Google Scholar	0.17×10^9	title, authors venue, year	title, authors venue, year
(P7)MOVIES	DBpedia	LinkedMDB	0.17×10^9	dbp:name dbo:director/dbp:name dbo:producer/dbp:name dbp:writer/dbp:name rdfs:label	dc2:title movie:director/movie:director_name movie:producer/movie:producer_name movie:writer/movie:writer_name rdfs:label

Coeficient	acadonto	acm.rkbexplorer	agrinepaldata	aims	alaska	apertium	arrayexpress	athelia	bfs.270a	biblioteca-nacional	brown	dblp	dbpedia	geonames	linkedgeodata	swdf	vivosearch	wiktionary	wordnet	yago
acadonto	1.0	0.02	0.11	0.05	0.00	0.03	0.02	0.06	0.01	0.02	0.02	0.02	0.00	0.02	0.00	0.01	0.01	0.02	0.01	0.02
acm.rkbexplorer	0.02	1.0	0.08	0.22	0.01	0.11	0.01	0.29	0.30	0.07	0.20	0.05	0.00	0.02	0.00	0.02	0.01	0.04	0.02	0.08
agrinepaldata	0.11	0.08	1.0	0.11	0.01	0.16	0.05	0.20	0.05	0.06	0.07	0.04	0.00	0.03	0.00	0.02	0.03	0.05	0.02	0.02
aims	0.05	0.22	0.11	1.0	0.02	0.07	0.08	0.36	0.27	0.08	0.12	0.08	0.00	0.04	0.00	0.06	0.06	0.03	0.03	0.10
alaska	0.00	0.01	0.01	0.02	1.0	0.01	0.00	0.02	0.01	0.01	0.01	0.01	0.00	0.00	0.00	0.01	0.02	0.01	0.01	0.07
apertium	0.03	0.11	0.16	0.07	0.01	1.0	0.02	0.05	0.06	0.06	0.07	0.08	0.00	0.05	0.00	0.02	0.02	0.10	0.04	0.20
arrayexpress	0.02	0.01	0.05	0.08	0.00	0.02	1.0	0.06	0.01	0.01	0.02	0.01	0.00	0.01	0.00	0.02	0.04	0.01	0.01	0.40
athelia	0.06	0.29	0.20	0.36	0.02	0.05	0.06	1.0	0.29	0.06	0.20	0.06	0.00	0.03	0.00	0.04	0.05	0.03	0.02	0.03
bfs.270a	0.01	0.30	0.05	0.27	0.01	0.06	0.01	0.29	1.0	0.06	0.15	0.03	0.00	0.01	0.00	0.02	0.02	0.02	0.02	0.02
biblioteca-nacional	0.02	0.07	0.06	0.08	0.01	0.06	0.01	0.06	0.06	1.0	0.08	0.05	0.00	0.00	0.00	0.03	0.01	0.04	0.02	0.05
brown	0.02	0.20	0.07	0.12	0.01	0.07	0.02	0.20	0.15	0.08	1.0	0.09	0.00	0.02	0.00	0.03	0.02	0.03	0.02	0.01
dblp	0.02	0.05	0.04	0.08	0.01	0.08	0.01	0.06	0.03	0.05	0.09	1.0	0.00	0.05	0.00	0.07	0.01	0.06	0.03	0.10
dbpedia	0.00	0.00	0.00	0.00	0.00	0.00	0.00	0.00	0.00	0.00	0.00	0.00	1.0	0.00	0.00	0.01	0.00	0.00	0.00	0.10
geonames	0.02	0.02	0.03	0.04	0.00	0.05	0.01	0.03	0.01	0.02	0.02	0.05	0.00	1.0	0.00	0.02	0.01	0.04	0.01	0.40
linkedgeodata	0.00	0.00	0.00	0.00	0.00	0.00	0.00	0.00	0.00	0.00	0.00	0.00	0.00	0.00	1.0	0.00	0.00	0.00	0.00	0.07
swdf	0.01	0.02	0.02	0.06	0.01	0.02	0.02	0.04	0.02	0.03	0.03	0.07	0.01	0.02	0.00	1.0	0.03	0.01	0.01	0.08
vivosearch	0.01	0.01	0.03	0.06	0.02	0.02	0.04	0.05	0.02	0.01	0.02	0.01	0.00	0.01	0.00	0.03	1.0	0.01	0.01	0.10
wiktionary	0.02	0.04	0.05	0.03	0.01	0.10	0.01	0.03	0.02	0.04	0.03	0.06	0.00	0.04	0.00	0.01	0.01	1.0	0.03	0.06
wordnet	0.01	0.02	0.02	0.03	0.01	0.04	0.01	0.02	0.02	0.02	0.02	0.03	0.00	0.01	0.00	0.01	0.01	0.03	1.0	0.04
yago	0.02	0.08	0.02	0.10	0.07	0.20	0.40	0.03	0.02	0.05	0.02	0.10	0.10	0.40	0.07	0.08	0.10	0.06	0.04	1.0

Table 15: Similarity table according to Jaccard method applied to a sample data, in which the level of similarity is also represented by the intensity of the color, as more intense color, as more similar are the datasets.

Coeficient	acadonto	acm.rkbexplorer	agrinepaldata	aims	alaska	apertium	arrayexpress	athelia	bfs.270a	biblioteca-nacional	brown	dblp	dbpedia	geonames	linkedgeodata	swdf	vivosearch	wiktionary	wordnet	yago
acadonto	1.0	0.04	0.16	0.20	0.00	0.04	0.24	0.16	0.04	0.04	0.04	0.04	0.00	0.04	0.04	0.08	0.20	0.04	0.04	0.04
acm.rkbexplorer	0.04	1.0	0.21	0.69	0.01	0.15	0.08	0.62	0.69	0.12	0.38	0.12	0.00	0.04	0.08	0.27	0.19	0.08	0.03	0.08
agrinepaldata	0.16	0.21	1.0	0.64	0.01	0.29	0.86	0.71	0.21	0.14	0.21	0.14	0.00	0.07	0.14	0.43	0.93	0.14	0.03	0.36
aims	0.20	0.69	0.64	1.0	0.02	0.08	0.10	0.43	0.36	0.09	0.16	0.22	0.00	0.05	0.05	0.07	0.32	0.10	0.06	0.17
alaska	0.00	0.01	0.01	0.02	1.0	0.01	0.01	0.02	0.02	0.01	0.01	0.01	0.00	0.00	0.02	0.02	0.05	0.01	0.01	0.01
apertium	0.04	0.15	0.29	0.08	0.01	1.0	0.02	0.20	0.27	0.13	0.20	0.10	0.00	0.13	0.20	0.02	0.40	0.13	0.04	0.27
arrayexpress	0.24	0.08	0.86	0.10	0.01	0.02	1.0	0.06	0.01	0.01	0.02	0.10	0.00	0.01	0.01	0.04	0.11	0.01	0.06	0.05
athelia	0.16	0.62	0.71	0.43	0.02	0.20	0.06	1.0	0.42	0.17	0.38	0.12	0.00	0.07	0.07	0.05	0.42	0.06	0.03	0.13
bfs.270a	0.04	0.69	0.21	0.36	0.02	0.27	0.01	0.42	1.0	0.08	0.21	0.07	0.10	0.04	0.06	0.03	0.13	0.06	0.03	0.04
biblioteca-nacional	0.04	0.12	0.14	0.09	0.01	0.13	0.01	0.17	0.08	1.0	0.12	0.07	0.00	0.04	0.09	0.03	0.22	0.06	0.03	0.13
brown	0.04	0.38	0.21	0.16	0.01	0.20	0.02	0.38	0.21	0.12	1.0	0.15	0.00	0.04	0.06	0.03	0.18	0.06	0.03	0.06
dblp	0.04	0.12	0.14	0.22	0.01	0.10	0.10	0.12	0.07	0.07	0.15	1.0	0.00	0.07	0.07	0.51	0.10	0.10	0.04	0.12
dbpedia	0.00	0.00	0.00	0.00	0.00	0.00	0.00	0.00	0.00	0.00	0.00	0.00	1.0	0.00	0.00	0.01	0.00	0.00	0.00	0.00
geonames	0.04	0.04	0.07	0.05	0.00	0.13	0.01	0.07	0.07	0.04	0.04	0.07	0.00	1.0	0.11	0.02	0.07	0.06	0.01	0.04
linkedgeodata	0.04	0.08	0.14	0.05	0.02	0.20	0.01	0.07	0.06	0.09	0.06	0.07	0.00	0.11	1.0	0.02	0.01	0.10	0.04	0.00
swdf	0.08	0.27	0.43	0.07	0.02	0.02	0.04	0.05	0.05	0.03	0.03	0.51	0.01	0.02	0.02	1.0	0.06	0.13	0.04	0.02
vivosearch	0.20	0.19	0.93	0.32	0.05	0.40	0.11	0.42	0.13	0.22	0.18	0.10	0.00	0.07	0.01	0.06	1.0	0.10	0.04	0.04
wiktionary	0.04	0.08	0.14	0.10	0.01	0.13	0.01	0.06	0.06	0.06	0.06	0.10	0.00	0.06	0.10	0.13	0.10	1.0	0.04	0.10
wordnet	0.04	0.03	0.03	0.06	0.01	0.04	0.01	0.06	0.03	0.03	0.03	0.04	0.00	0.01	0.04	0.04	0.04	0.04	1.0	0.04
yago	0.10	0.08	0.10	0.10	0.01	0.10	0.15	0.13	0.14	0.21	0.04	0.05	0.19	0.01	0.20	0.13	0.09	0.00	0.05	1.0

Table 16: A sample of how much a dataset in contained in each other, in which the level of containment is also represented by the intensity of the color, as more intense color, as more contained are the datasets.

Dataset	#ExactMatch	#sim > 0.8	#PropClass
swdf	22	64	288
yago	6	65	373546
dblp	6	9	41
linkedgeodata	5	617	11799
wiktionary	4	6	31
geonames	4	12	27
wordnet	3	26	69
wikidata	0	5	427
freebase	0	55	17587

Table 17: Top 10 datasets containing exact the same URI and containing the most similar URIs according to our similarity approach, in which #PropClass represents the total number of properties and classes from the dataset.

#Datasets	#DsropMatch	time (seconds)	#triples	Synthetic
3	2	1	11	Yes
10	7	2	1198508	no
100	39	12	7996408	no
200	92	40	22982984	no
300	135	57	34792121	no
400	186	73	43864522	no
500	229	87	54227780	no
600	291	425	85041239	no

Table 18: Evaluation on the Match algorithm, where **DsPropMatch** refers to the number of properties/classes the datasets share among each other.

CONSISTENCY IN LARGE AMOUNT OF RDF SOURCES

5

Inconsistency on datasets and links among them leads us to terrible mistakes, in order to avoid them we start with an approach to tackle the heterogeneity in DBpedia Identifiers[VAK15], than we developed an approach to find e rroneous l inks i n a l arge a mount of RDF sources[VSN17a].

This chapter aims merge 2 publications, [VAK15] and [VSN17a], startin by tackling heterogeneity in DBpedia identifier followed by an approach to find erroneous links in large amount of RDF sources.

5.1 CONSISTENCY IN HETEROGENEOUS DBPEDIA IDENTIFIERS

In this part of the book, we cover the RQ4 having a practical case with DBpedia improving the quality of the identifiers in order to better relate the datasets. We approach a problem where the DBpedia dataset has multiple URIs within the dataset and from other datasets connected with (transitive) `owl:sameAs` relations and thus referring to the same concepts. With this heterogeneity of identifiers it is complicated for users and agents to find t he u nique identifier which should be preferably used. We are introducing the concept of DBpedia Unique Identifier (DUI) and a dataset of linksets relating URIs to DUIs. In order to improve the quality of our dataset we developed a mechanism that allows the user to rate and suggest links. As proof of concept an implementation with a graphical web user interface is provided for accessing the linkset and rating the links. The DBpedia sameAs service is available .

5.1.1 *The DBpediaSameAs approach*

As DBpedia [LIJ$^+$14] was evolving during the 9 years of its existence, the community extended the linksets to DBpedia resources. Thus, DBpedia has more than one URI that represents the same resource, which leads to the identifier heterogeneity problem. For instance a DBpedia resource can contain `owl:sameAs` links to other data sets such as FreeBase[1], Wikidata, GeoNames[2] or yago[3].

Further DBpedia has more than one URI representing the same resource within the dataset, e.g. the `dbpedia:Brassil` has at least the following equivalents within the DBpedia `dbpedia:Republica_Federativa_do_Brasil`, `dbpedia:ISO_3166-1:BR` and `dbpedia:Brazil` which are all redirecting to `dbpedia:Brazil`. Thus a problem to consider is to directly resolve any of the equivalents directly to the final URI e.g. without any redundancies.

Also, according to Halpin et. al. [HHM$^+$10] and Wood et. al. [WZRH14], *sameas.org* has collected millions of triples with `owl:same As` relations. It would be important to promote reciprocal owl:sameAs confirmation mechanisms and develop effective trust mechanisms to assure the quality of `owl:sameAs` relations.

To tackle the identifier heterogeneity problem we are making the following contributions:

- We describe an approach for the mitigation of the identifier heterogeneity problem and implement a prototype where the user is able to evaluate existing links, as well as suggest new links to be rated.

- The ability to generate statistics about good and bad links which, brings the possibility to have a quality control for the links to DBpedia.

- We define the DBpedia Unique Identifier (DUI), which instead of several transient `owl:sameAs` DBpedia URIs for the same final address, now is possible to have a unique URI from DBpedia. A DUI goes directly to the final address instead of having to process several possible intermediate results. For example, with a URI from *Freebase*, 17 redundant URIs from DBpedia where avoided or if one used a service such as sameAs.org, 1141 URIs would be avoided.

The rest of the chapter is organized as follows: section 5.1.2 represents a proposed approach for tackling the identifier heterogeneity problem and section 5.1.5 we evaluate our work.

5.1.2   *Representation of the idea*

This section provides an explanation about our main idea, such as implementation and descriptions.

Before continuing the work, there are some definitions that were adopted.

- **Normalization of the URI**: Is understood by normalizing URIs, the fact of eliminating redundancies.

- **DBpedia unique identifier**: The DBpedia Unique Identifier (DUI) is an unique URI that identifies a resource in the DBpedia repository and also is the result of our normalization.

The idea started with a stand alone service on the web that solves the problem where the user provides a URI as parameter and instead of several transient URIs with `owl:sameAs` property, the user receives a single DUI from our service.

5.1.3   *The work-flow*

The work-flow for requesting the DUI of a given resource is represented in figure 19. Firstly, the user will provide a URI from some address, i.e. FreeBase. Then, instead of possible several results of URIs with the property `owl:sameAs`, our system will return a DUI. Consequently, the user has a possibility to rate, verify, validate, and suggest a different link. Then the rate can give us a chance to have statistics about the quality of the links.

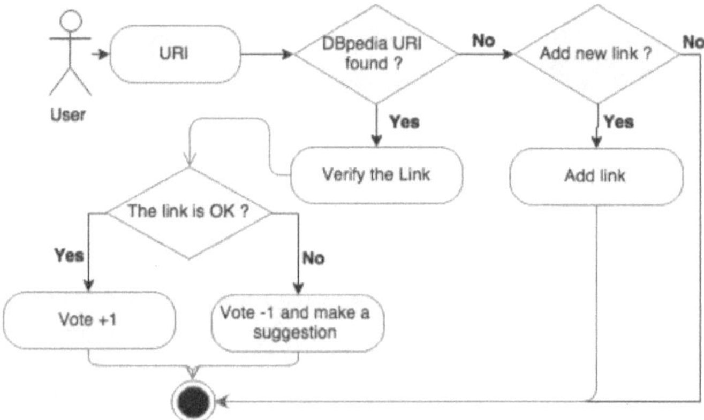

Figure 19: General work-flow.

A service, also was implemented, where the user can provide a URI and the API will return the DBpedia identifier like a URI that represents the `owl:sameAs` about the URI provided.

5.1.4   *Methodology*

This section describes in four steps the technique and how the idea was developed, from phase of importing links to a relational database until the development of the service on the web and a GUI.

(1) The files with triples that contains `owl:sameAs` links, were downloaded. (2) All triples were imported in a relational database [4], because we will use some characteristics of a relational database i.e. comparative with voting system in future works. (3) An implementation of a service on the web was provided, where the user enters the URI and receives a DUI. (4) In order to provide an interface to

access this service were created a web system that receive as input a URI, return as output an DBpedia identifier and allow rate and make suggestions about the resulting link.

figure 20 presents the relation of the contribution in a graph form.

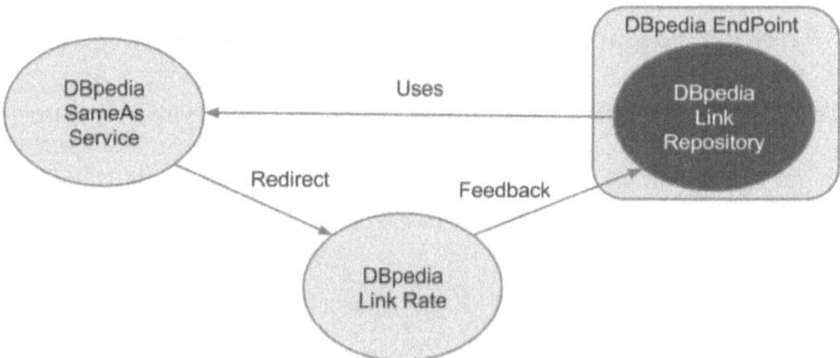

Figure 20: Relation of the contributions.

Where the DBpedia Link Repository uses the DBpediaSameAs service in order to tackle the heterogeneity and giving the appropriate DUI, that redirects the user to the DBpedia Link Rate interface, thus, providing a feedback to the DBpedia Link Repository, therefore, improving the quality of the DBpedia endpoint.

5.1.5 *Evaluation*

The aim of this qualitative evaluation was centered in verifying the behavior of the service DBpediaSameAs, the Graphical User Interface (GUI) that gives the possibility to verify and rate the links.

There are chosen 3 evaluation criteria:

(1) **Normalization on DBpedia URIs:** With this criteria was evaluated if the DBpediaSameAs can provide an normalization on DBpedia URIs. (2) **Rate the Links:** Where was evaluated if the DBpediaSameAs can provide a way to rate the links. (3) **DBpediaSameAs as service:** Was evaluated if DBpediaSameAs can provide a stand alone service on the web that brings the normalization on DBpedia URIs.

5.1.6 *Normalization on DBpedia URIs*

The criteria used in this evaluation are uniquely to tackle heterogeneity, that was observed during the search of co-references between different data sets with a problem about redundancies.

When was used a URI from freebase in order to obtain a DBpedia URI was observed that at least 3 URIs were returned, that drives to the same final address.

As an example of a real case, executed in our public server, with a URI from Freebase:

```
1
     freebase.com%2Fns%2Fm.015fr
2

3
```

Where, in this case, instead of 17 URIs from DBpedia, that goes to the same final address, our approach drives the user directly to the final address.

As can be observed on the figure 22 that approach the transitive and redirect URIs, where show that with this approach instead of have several URIs the user can have only one from the DBpediaSameAs. Thus, in this way, providing a normalization on DBpedia URIs.

5.1.7 *Rate the links*

In order to have a link rating, were implemented a GUI that allows the users to give some feedback, suggestions, in this way, improving the quality of the links. The rate is a quite simple process, the GUI just ask the user to rate the link with +1 if the link attends your expectations or -1 if the link is wrong or some type of spam. The GUI was developed using concepts from prefix.cc [5] and work from Zaveri[ZKS[+]13] such our system of rate (+1 and -1) and the standard of the web documents. Some improvements and personalization, also was provided, such as the suggestions and the possibility to check the link. The figure 21 shows the moment when the user clicked on the -1 and indicated that the user didn't like the link and was asked to make a suggestion of a new URI.

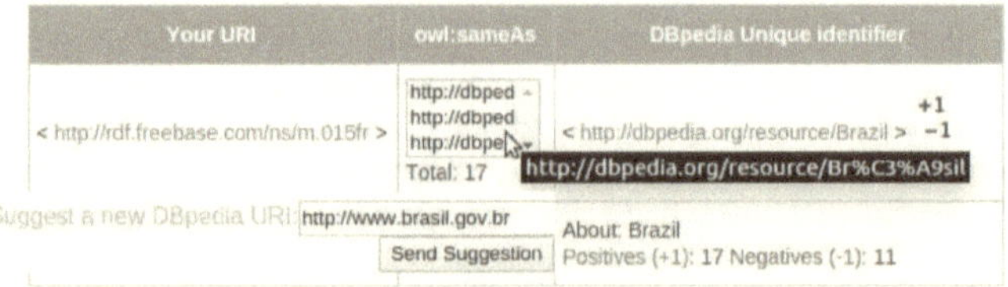

Figure 21: Rate a link.

The field about a suggestion for a new link will only appear when the user are not satisfied with the current link, then, when clicking on the -1, then the system will ask for an optional suggestion.

5.1.8 *Results*

The results of this work could also be expressed in numbers that was obtained during importing triples to the relational database and with some results from the sameAs.org web site. A total of 62,531,487 triples imported into our database, the time was 2,220 seconds for the whole operation, thus, was noticed that 28,167 triples were imported per second. The source code used to obtain the results is available in our github repository[6].

Transitive and Redirect Links

Transitive and Redirect Links are redundancies at DBpedia that supposed has a link to the same place, in other words, they use `owl:sameAs` property, this links will redirect another links, will provide a transition between the links, that's why the name transitive. In this case, instead of using this transitive links that points to the same final destination URI, this final destination URI will be used directly. The figure 22 try to make more clear this explanation.

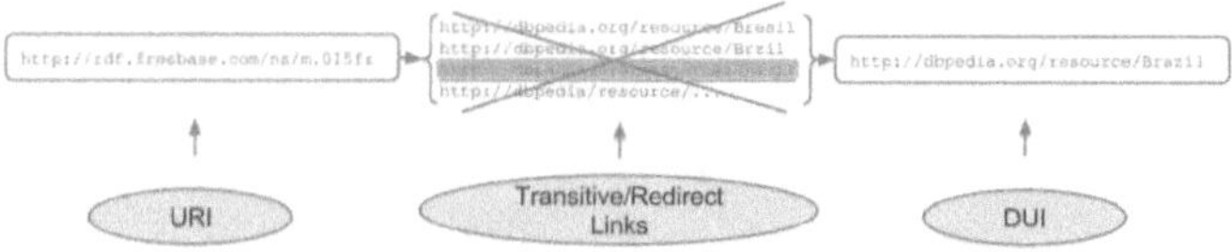

Figure 22: Transitive / Redirect links in DBpedia.

Was discovered and treated 6,473,988 triples with transitive and redirect links from 62,531,487 imported links among 142 domains inside DBpedia. Then, 10.35% of the links can be avoided in some cases.

5.1.9 *Discussion*

The DBpediaSameAs was evaluated with its normalization of URIs, link rate, and DBpediaSameAs as a stand alone service on the web. As results of the normalization a DUI was obtained in order to tackle the heterogeneity. In other words, instead of several URIs e.g. from sameAs.org one DUI was obtained. The link rate functionality further allows to improve the quality of the dataset.

Despite, the GUI of DBpediaSameAs, also a stand alone service on the web was developed that brings the functionality to get a DUI without a GUI for agents or people which don't need to use the DBpediaSameAs in a Graphical mode, allowing use as an off-the-shelf component.

5.2 CONSISTENCY IN LARGE-SCALE RDF SOURCES: DETECTION OF ERRONEOUS LINKS

This part of the book shows an extension of the previous work[VAK15] and cover the RQ5, in which we discuss the importance of the links for the Linked Data Web as they make a large number of tasks possible, including cross-ontology, question answering and federated queries. However, a large number of these links are erroneous and can thus lead to these applications producing absurd results. We present a time-efficient a nd c omplete a pproach f or t he d etection of erroneous links for properties that are transitive. To this end, we make use of the semantics of URIs on the Data Web and combine it with an efficient g raph p artitioning a lgorithm. We t hen a pply our algorithm to the LinkLion repository and show that we can analyze 19,200,114 links in 4.6 minutes. Our results show that at least 13% of the `owl:sameAs` links we considered are erroneous. In addition, our analysis of the provenance of links allows discovering agents and knowledge bases that commonly display poor linking. Our algorithm can be easily executed in parallel and on a GPU. We show that these implementations are up to two orders of magnitude faster than classical reasoners and a non-parallel implementation.

5.2.1 *The CEDAL approach*

Links across knowledge bases play a fundamental role in Linked Data [AP13] as they allow users to navigate across datasets, integrate Linked Data sources [NSL14], perform federated queries [SNP+13] across data sources and perform large-scale inference on the data. Given the importance of links, corresponding repositories such as *sameas.org*[7] and LinkLion [NSNR14b] (of which *sameas.org* is a subset) have been created. In addition to facilitating the finding o f l inks between resources and knowledge bases, these repositories also allow detecting significant e rrors a cross l inks. F or e xample, a ccording to LinkLion and by virtue of transitivity, the resources `orca:21075` and `orca:1946`[8] stand for the same entity of the real world but have different URIs within the same knowledge base. This clearly goes against the definition o f U RIs a s u sed i n R DF. fi gure 29 sh ows a fictional example to help illustrate such problems, which can be classified as **contradiction problems**, according to the quality dimension of consistency [ZRM+15]. In our example, we can infer that one of the links along the path that led to this inference is wrong or that the knowledge base in itself contains an error. While such errors can be potentially detected by computing the closure of equivalence links using the characteristics of equivalence relations and an inference engine,

our experiments with Pellet [BHJV] – the fastest inference engine to
the best of our knowledge – suggest that inference engines do not
scale to the millions of links found on the Web of Data.

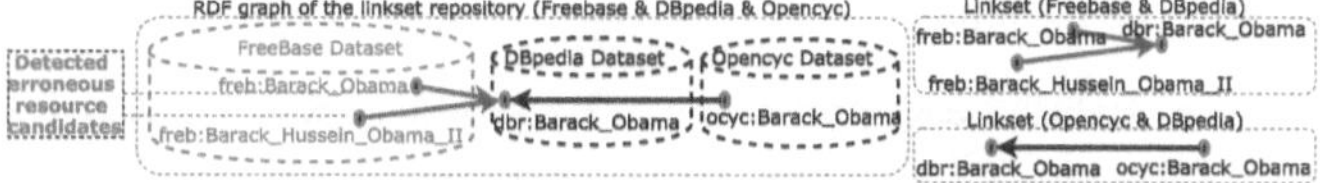

Figure 23: Manual detection of erroneous resource candidates.

The poor performance on closure computations is also known from
literature (see, e.g., [AGP08]). For instance, the computation of closures in RDF graphs has several drawbacks. Firstly, it is known that
the **size** of the transitive closure of a graph G is of **quadratic order**
in the worst case, making the computation and storage of the closure
too expensive for web-scale applications. Secondly, once the transitive closure has been computed, all queries are evaluated over a data
source which can be much larger than the original one. This can be
particularly **inefficient for queries** that must scan a large part of the
input data.

Our intuition is that it is actually not necessary to compute the closures; instead, we can use adjacency lists and create graph partitions
based on an algorithm called *Union Find* [Tar75]. Therewith, we obtain a solution with a time complexity that is decreased from $O(n^2)$
to $O(m \log n)$, where m is the number of operations (either *Union* or
Find) that are applied to n elements.

In this paper, we aim to find erroneous links across knowledge
bases by reusing the uniqueness of the semantics of URIs within given
knowledge bases. We hence present a novel time-efficient algorithm
called *Consistency Error Detection Algorithm* Consistency Error Detection Algorithm (CEDAL), in which the error detection consists of finding distinct resources (i.e., resources with distinct URIs) which share
the same dataset, given an RDF graph representing the union of all
knowledge bases in a link repository.

With our work, we address the following research questions:

1. Is there a time-efficient algorithm to detect erroneous links in
   large-scale link repositories?

2. Is there an approach to discover whether a linkset[9] is consistent
   without computing all closures required by the property axiom?

The contributions of this work are listed below:

- A time-efficient algorithm for the detection of erroneous links
  in large-scale link repositories without computing all closures
  required by the property axiom.

---

9 We refer to the definition of linkset as defined in the W3C document

- An approach that brings the possibility to track the consistency problems inside link repositories.

- A scalable algorithm that works well in a parallel and non-parallel mode.

- A study case applied to a link repository called LinkLion.

- A new linkset quality measure based on the number of erroneous candidates.

The remainder of this chapter is structured as follows: section 5.2.2 presents our algorithm for the detection of erroneous links in large-scale link repositories; section 5.2.3 presents the error types and a quality measure for linksets; section 5.2.4 presents the evaluation of our approach.

5.2.2 *Method*

After introducing the terminology and symbolism used in this work, in this section, we present our error detection algorithm.

Error Detection algorithm

Our algorithm targets consistency errors in large-scale link repositories. We assume a union of linksets $\mathcal{L}$ as given input. The aim is to find cases in which equivalent resources (according to the OWL semantics) in $\mathcal{L}$ share the same dataset. The basic intuition here is equivalent resources (i.e., resources that stand for the same entity from the real world) being in one knowledge base is a clear hint towards (1) an error in the knowledge base itself or (2) an error during the generation of the links that allowed generating this equivalence.

In figure 24, we show how our algorithm works. Given datasets $D_1, ..., D_n$, resources $R = \{a, b, c, d, e, f\}$, the idea is to detect two or more resources sharing the same dataset inside the same cluster, following the steps described in the following list and into the algorithm 4.

1. As input, the algorithm receives a set of linksets $L = \{(r_1, r_2), ..., (r_n, r_m)\}$, where r_n represents the resources.

2. The linksets are merged creating a unique RDF graph $\mathcal{L} = \bigcup_i L_i$, where $L_i = (s, p, o) : s \in D_i^{(s)}, o \in D_i^{(t)}$, D represents source and target datasets of the linksets and (s, p, o) are subject, predicate and object of an RDF triple.

3. From $\mathcal{L}$, create clusters $\mathcal{C}$, containing the resources, datasets and the knowledge base.

4. Find cases in which two or more resources r_i belong to the same dataset D.

5. Put these resources, related paths, dataset names and knowledge-bases into a list and return this list $\mathcal{O}$.

6. The output are all paths that were considered wrong and the original mappings.

Our algorithm works by partitioning a graph inside an adjacency list that contains: (1) An array per vertex for a total of V arrays, where we are only considering the space for the array pointer, not the contents of the array. (2) Each directed edge is contained once somewhere in the adjacency list, for a total of E edges, where a bidirectional edge is just 2 directed edges, assuming we are using bi-directional edges.

In this context we are using techniques from an well know algorithm called Union-Find, where the definition in computer science, is based in a disjoint-set data structure, also called a merge–find set, is a data structure that keeps track of a set of elements partitioned into a number of disjoint (non overlapping) subsets. It supports two useful operations:

(1)Find: Determine which subset a particular element is in. Find typically returns an item from this set that serves as its "representative"; by comparing the result of two Find operations, one can determine whether two elements are in the same subset.

(2)Union: Join two subsets into a single subset.

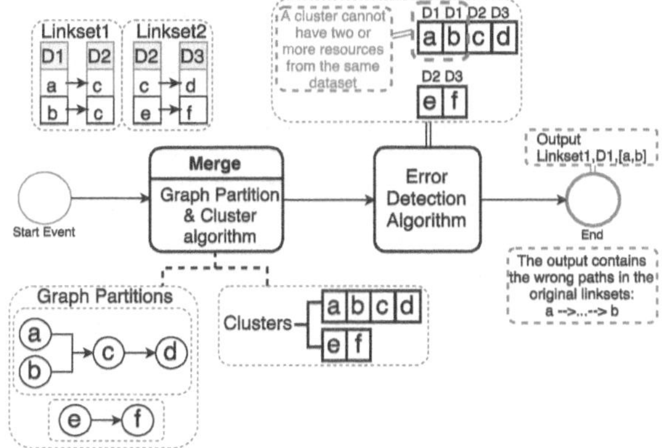

Figure 24: Error detection.

Problem statement.

We formalize the problem of *detection of erroneous links in large-scale link repositories* as follows.

Algorithm 4 Consistency Error Detection Algorithm (CEDAL)

Input: $L : L_i = (s,p,o) : s \in D_i^{(s)}, o \in D_i^{(t)}$
Output: An error list with erroneous nodes.

```
 1: procedure CEDAL(G(V, E))
 2:     P = getPartitions(G(V, E))
 3:     for all p ∈ P do (in parallel)
 4:         for all r ∈ p do push onto clusterDataset r, MapResourcesDataset.get(r)
 5:         end for
 6:         for all r ∈ clusterDataset do
 7:             if countDataset(r) > 1 then push onto ErrorList re-
    source.originalFileName + resource.dataset + resource.path
 8:             end if
 9:         end for
10:     end for
11:     return ErrorList
12: end procedure
13: procedure GETPARTITIONS(G(V, E))
14:     for all v ∈ V do
15:         push onto
16: MapResourcesDataset v, extracDataset(v)t
17:         push all nodes connected to v onto V        ▷ UnionFind algorithm
18:         push V onto P
19:     end for
20:     return P
21: end procedure
```

From this section on, we will refer to the union of all linksets as $\mathcal{L} = \bigcup_i L_i$, the set of all datasets as $\mathcal{D}$, the clusters (or graph partitions) as $\mathcal{C}$, the candidates (i.e., set of resources belonging to the same dataset) $\mathcal{P}$. A linkset $L \in \mathcal{L}$ contains triples (or links) (s, p, o) such as:

$$(s, p, o) \in L : s \in D_i, o \in D_j, i \neq j \tag{22}$$

Each candidate P abides by the following restriction:

$$\forall r_i, r_j \in P : r_i \neq r_j \Rightarrow (r_i, x, r_j) \in \mathcal{L}^* \vee (r_j, x, r_i) \in \mathcal{L}^* \tag{23}$$

where x is a property (e.g., `owl:sameAs`). In other words, each element in P is linked to at least another element in the set. Candidates are assigned one of two classes, positive (i.e., candidates with errors) or negative. The positive cases are represented as follows.

$$P \in \mathcal{P}^+ \iff (\exists r_1 \in P \cap D_1, r_2 \in P \cap D_2) \therefore D_1 = D_2 \Rightarrow r_1 \neq r_2 \tag{24}$$

The negative cases are defined in the following equation.

$$P \in \mathcal{P}^- \iff (\forall r_1 \in P \cap D_1, r_2 \in P \cap D_2) \therefore D_1 = D_2 \Rightarrow r_1 = r_2 \tag{25}$$

The target is thus to find the set of erroneous candidates $\mathcal{P}^+$. As shown in the next section, we cannot state that a link connecting these resources is wrong, but we can state that the error lies somewhere between the links that connect them and the organization of the dataset they belong to.

5.2.3 Error Types and Quality Measure for Linkset Repositories

The application of the two measures requires the output from CEDAL, allowing to identify two types of errors among the erroneous candidates from the output.

Error Types

We identified two types of errors, in which can be defined in quality dimensions by [ZRM⁺15]. (1) **Semantic accuracy** errors, in which we detect if data values correctly represent the real world facts. (2) **Consistency** and **Conciseness** errors where a knowledge base is free of logical or formal contradictions concerning particular knowledge representation and inference mechanisms and the minimization of redundancy of entities at the schema and the data level. figure 25 shows a fictional example of both error types, in which we represent links between GeoNames[10] and DBpedia.[11]

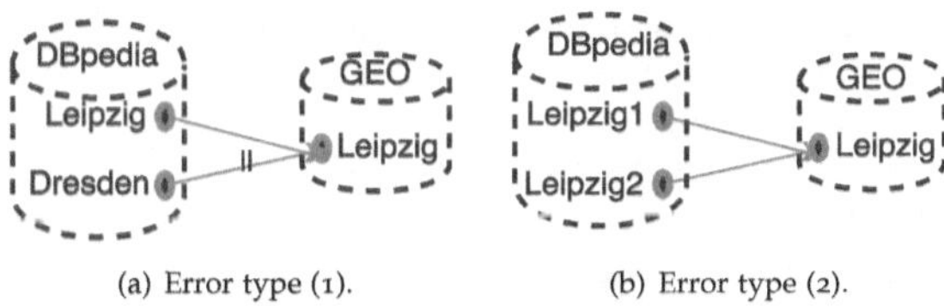

(a) Error type (1).   (b) Error type (2).

Figure 25: Detected error types.

In this example, figure 25(a) shows an error of type (1), in which an erroneous `owl:sameAs` link between the city of Dresden and the city of Leipzig was detected. The figure 25(b) shows an error of type (2) where the resource about the city of Leipzig is duplicated within the DBpedia dataset.

We manually analyzed a random sample of the errors. Among 100 occurrences, 90% are of type (2). It was not feasible in practice to perform this evaluation in an automatic way, due to the fact that it involves semantic accuracy and thus needs human feedback. Moreover, some URIs are unreachable, resulting many times in *timeout errors*, such as HTTP 404, 500 and 503 errors.[12] In summary, it was not practicable to automatically distinguish these types of errors among the erroneous candidates detected by CEDAL.

Quality Measure

Based on the error types from CEDAL, we present three linkset quality measures, evaluating the information accessed by cross-walking the linksets of LinkLion.

The **Semantic Accuracy of linksets** indicates whether the data values from the RDF links represent real world facts. **Example:** Let us assume that we have a linkset from DBpedia and Geonames. A link `<dbr:dresden owl:sameAs geo:leipzig>` would clearly be inaccurate, since Dresden and Leipzig are two different cities.

The **consistency and conciseness of links** inform whether a linkset is free of logical or formal contradictions with respect to particular knowledge representation and inference mechanisms and the minimization of redundancy of resources that belongs to the same dataset inside a linkset repository. **Example:** With a linkset from DBpedia and Geonames, let us assume we found two links represented by `<dbr:leipzig1 owl:sameAs geo:leipzig>` and `<dbr:leipzig2 owl:sameAs geo:leipzig>`. Since `dbr:leipzig1` and `dbr:leipzig2` belong to the same dataset, this characterizes a redundancy and it contradicts the assumption that two URIs in a dataset cannot stand for the same thing from the real world.

In order to evaluate data quality in linksets, on the lines of the works summarized in the Data Quality survey [ZRM$^+$15], we propose three new metrics:

M1: Rate of consistent resources inside linkset repositories.

> Let us consider a candidate $P \in \mathcal{P}$ containing only resources which belong to the same dataset. The rate of consistent candidates is defined as follows:

$$M1 = \frac{\sum_{P \in \mathcal{P}^-} |P|}{\sum_{P \in \mathcal{P}} |P|} \qquad (26)$$

> where $\mathcal{P}^-$ is the set of consistent (i.e., non-erroneous) candidates. We call M1 the **consistency index**.

M2: Rate of candidates in $\mathcal{P}$ containing resources whose internal links are real world facts. Let us introduce a function $f(s, p, o)$ which expresses the verification of a triple (s, p, o) in the real world, assuming value 1 if the statements holds true and 0 otherwise. This metric addresses errors of type (1).

$$M2 = \frac{|\{P \in \mathcal{P}^+ : \forall r_i, r_j \in P \; r_i \neq r_j \Rightarrow f(r_i, p, r_j) = 1\}| + |\mathcal{P}^-|}{|\mathcal{P}|} \qquad (27)$$

M3: Rate of candidates in $\mathcal{P}$ which are free of redundant resources. This metric addresses errors of type (2).

$$M3 = \frac{|\{P \in \mathcal{P}^+ : \exists r_i, r_j \in P \; r_i \neq r_j \Rightarrow f(r_i, p, r_j) = 0\}| + |\mathcal{P}^-|}{|\mathcal{P}|} \qquad (28)$$

As can be seen, M2 and M3 are dependent on each other.

In this paper, we focus on the computation of M1. Although M2 and M3 are left for future research, we included them to encourage their evaluation and use.

5.2.4 *Evaluation*

To verify our hypothesis, in this section we show that CEDAL brings an efficient way to track the erroneous candidates inside large-scale linkset repositories.

5.2.5 *Experimental setup*

As our study case, we use a linkset repository called LinkLion [NSNR14b] due to some advantages such as provenance, linksets from the most used datasets, i.e. DBpedia, Yago and Opencyc, where the users are empowered to upload links and specify how these were created. Moreover, users and applications can select and download sets of links via dumps or SPARQL queries.

The table 24 shows that 99.9% of links from LinkLion are owl:sameAs links, amounting to 19,200,114 triples. Thus, in our experiments we are using only owl:sameAs links.

Table 19: Link types

Property	Triples
sameAs	19,606,657 (with duplicates)
country	1,309
author	766
spokenIn	624
locatedIn	250
exactMatch	167
near	30
spatial#P	28
seeAlso	14
organism	14
made	4

The experiments were performed using two configurations: (1) a laptop with Intel Core i7, 8 GB RAM, a video card NVIDIA NVS4200, Operational System MS Windows 10 and Java SE Development Kit 8. (2) An Intel Xeon Core i7 processor with 40 cores, 128 GB RAM on an Ubuntu 14.04.5 LTS with Java SE Development Kit 8. The results including the output file for LinkLion are available online. The total number of 19.6million links was processed by our algorithm in 4.6 minutes with the configuration (2). The total amount of errors were $1,352,366$ of candidates, where the total amount of domains were 254 and the number of linkset files was 553, where 48.3% of these knowledge base files has less than 10 resources detected as erroneous candidates.

Ranking the erroneous candidates

To evaluate how effective CEDAL is, we create a score in order to rank the erroneous candidates based on the number of detected resources with errors, in which the table 20, show two fictional examples of tuples in the same pattern of the output from CEDAL.

Table 20: Fictional example results.

Knowledge-base	Data-set domain	$\mathbb{C}$	μ
Linkset1.nt	Data-set1	URI1,URI2	1
Linkset2.nt	Data-set2	URI1,URI2,URI3,URI4	6

The μ score is calculated by $\mu = \frac{|\mathbb{C}|(|\mathbb{C}|-1)}{2}$, in which we use the cardinality of $\mathbb{C}$ representing the detected erroneous candidates. The figures 30 and 26(b) shows the top 5 erroneous candidates according to the rank score.

Table 21: Legend for the figures 30 and 26(b)

Label	Knowledge Base
K1	dotac.rkbexplorer.com—eprints.rkbexplorer.com.nt
K2	d-nb.info—viaf.org.nt
K3	dblp.rkbexplorer.com—dblp.l3s.de.nt
K4	linkedgeodata.org—sws.geonames.org.nt
K5	citeseer.rkbexplorer.com—kisti.rkbexplorer.com.nt
K6	wiki.rkbexplorer.com—oai.rkbexplorer.com.nt
K7	www4.wiwiss.fu-berlin.de—dbpedia.org.nt
K8	southampton.rkbexplorer.com—nsf.rkbexplorer.com.nt
K9	rae2001.rkbexplorer.com—newcastle.rkbexplorer.com.nt
K10	lod.geospecies.org—bio2rdf.org.nt

Considering only linksets between different datasets, the knowledge-base with more errors comes from the links in

```
dotac.rkbexplorer.com - eprints.rkbexplorer.com
```

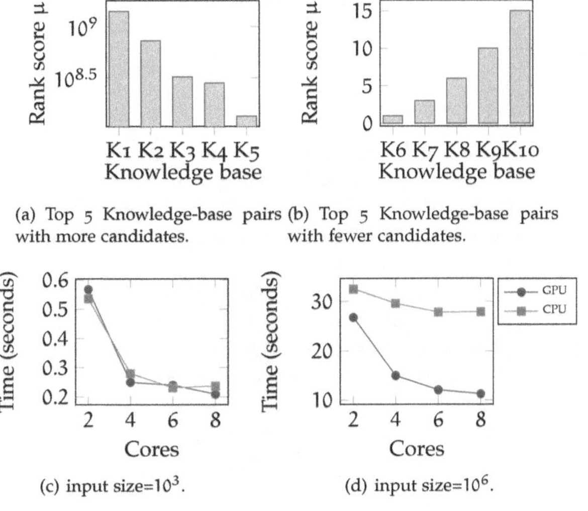

(a) Top 5 Knowledge-base pairs with more candidates.

(b) Top 5 Knowledge-base pairs with fewer candidates.

(c) input size=10^3.

(d) input size=10^6.

Figure 26: Error rank (legends: see table 21) and Runtime results according to the input size, CPU and GPU.

with $458,324$ links per mapping[13], in which we found $53,074$ erroneous resource candidates resulting in a score of $1,408,398,201$. The knowledge base with fewer errors comes from the links in

```
lod.geospecies.org - bio2rdf.org.nt
```

with $9,723$ links per mapping, in which we found 6 erroneous resource candidates and a score of 15, also 193 datasets with no errors at all.

Runtime experiments

The experiments were performed with the input size varying between 10^3 and 10^6 RDF triples using the configuration (1), as shown in figures 26(c) and 26(d). Our algorithm processed all $19,200,114$ links from LinkLion in 4.6 minutes with the configuration (2). The results indicate that our algorithm scales well to large links repositories and can also be adapted to the hardware on which it is executed. For example, it can be easily implemented to make use of benefits of CPUs and GPUs.

Scalability Evaluation

Our algorithm performs well in parallel and non-parallel environments. The performance of our algorithm improved in accordance to the number of CPUs, showing that our algorithm is scalable, performing well with large linksets with size more than 10^6 as shown in figures 26(c) and 26(d).

Parallel Implementation

Our algorithm implementation contains parallel code snippets in which we perform a load-and-balance of the data among CPU/GPU cores when available. This specific characteristic offers the possibility for utilization when hardware for parallel computing is available, such as CPU/GPU processors.

To illustrate this part of our idea, we can state: Given a graph $G(V, E)$, that contains all linksets from the repository $G(V, E) \subseteq \mathcal{L}$, this graph has partitions $P \subset G(V, E)$. Thus, errors are calculated for each partition, the processes are separated in threads and these threads are spread among CPU/GPU cores. Thus, we process the graph partitions in parallel, as shown in figure 27.

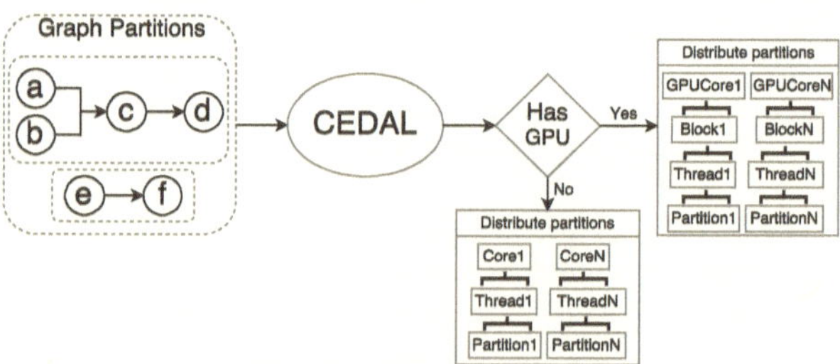

Figure 27: CEDAL CPU/GPU processing

Consistency by provenance of links

Thanks to the information found in LinkLion, we are able to check the provenance of links. This allowed us to analyze them more in details by finding which link discovery framework has created the link. The links were generated by four types of frameworks: *LIMES* [NA11a], *SILK* [VBGK09], *DBpedia Extraction Framework* [LIJ$^+$15] and *sameas.org*[14]. The type of links provided by *sameas.org* were generated into human-curated knowledge bases, such as DBpedia (which is based on Wikipedia), Freebase, and OpenCyc.

We found a 13.5% error rate from *sameas.org* versus a 4.1% error rate of the algorithms such as *LIMES* [NA11a]. They are all below 5% as table 22 shows; column Errors represents the rate of all resources belonging to error candidates and column M1 represents the respective quality measure.

Table 22: Comparison of results with respect to the provenance of the links.

Framework	Errors	Resources	Errors (%)	M1
sameas.org	3,792,326	28,130,994	13.5	0.865
LIMES	1,130	27,819	4.1	0.951
Silk	5,933	208,300	2.8	0.972
DBpedia Extraction Framework	12,615	914,180	1.4	0.986
All frameworks	3,812,004	29,281,293	13.0	0.870

According to this data, we can say that algorithms such as LIMES, SILK, and the DBpedia Extraction Framework have a higher consistency index than *sameas.org*. This might be explained by the fact that no mechanism of link validation is present on *sameas.org*.

Comparison with other works

To the best of our knowledge, CEDAL is the first approach that aims to detect the consistency of RDF link repositories. However, the problem that CEDAL addresses can be solved in other ways. One alternative to solving our problem is to use reasoning. However, this approach requires the computation of all closures required by the property axiom. To check whether our approach performs better than a closure-based approach, we compared CEDAL with an algorithm for computing closures – dubbed Closure Generator – without using a reasoner and with Pellet, which is considered the state-of-the-art reasoner [BHJV]. figure 28 shows that CEDAL is significantly faster than Pellet, reaching up to three orders of magnitude of speedup when faced with 10^6 triples. This result can be partly explained by Pellet also checks the knowledge base for every single coherence and consistency axiom. However, we did not need such an in-depth analysis.

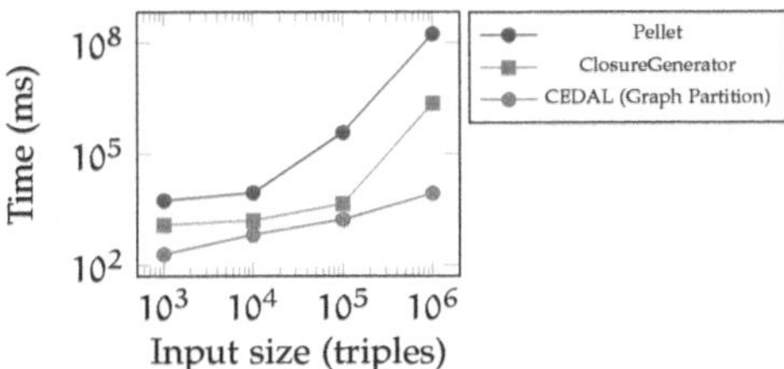

Figure 28: Pellet vs. ClosureGenerator vs. CEDAL

5.3 DETECTING ERRONEOUS LINK CANDIDATES IN EDUCATIONAL LINK REPOSITORIES

This part of the book complements this work presenting an application of CEDAL[VSN17a], detecting erroneous links in Educational datasets, presenting two more research questions related to RQ5.

Interlinking educational datasets is a challenging task when the majority of data is not organized in a Linked Data standards. Thus, we face data that is not well interlinked among several different datasets of the educational area. This task usually involves many steps such as Link Discovery, where links across homogeneous datasets are discovered and stored, and quality assessment of these links, where the consistency of these links is verified. H owever, a l arge n umber of these links are erroneous and can thus lead to these applications producing absurd results. The aim of this paper is to provide a way to check the consistency of linksets from Educational area. To this end, we are using an approach called CEDAL which is a time-efficient and complete approach for the detection of erroneous links for properties that are transitive. In order to evaluate our approach we selected $1,049$ transitive from linksets from Nature.com, Geonames, educational Programs, among others.

5.3.1 *The CEDAL education approach*

Links across knowledge bases play a fundamental role in Linked Data [AP13] as they allow users to navigate across datasets, integrate Linked Data sources [NSL14], perform federated queries [SNP+13] across data sources and perform large-scale inference on the data. Given the importance of links, corresponding repositories such as *nature.com*[15] and LinkLion [NSNR14b] have been created. In addition to facilitating the finding o f l inks between resources and knowledge bases, these repositories also allow detecting significant e rrors a cross l inks. F or e xample, according to Nature.com and by virtue of transitivity, the resources. `ExpressionCollection` and `Collection` stand for the same entity of the real world but have different URIs within the same knowledge base. This clearly goes against the definition of URIs as used in RDF.

figure 29 shows a fictional example to help illustrate such problems, which can be classified as **contradiction problems**, according to the quality dimension of consistency [ZRM+15]. In our example, we can infer that one of the links along the path that led to this inference is wrong or that the knowledge base in itself contains an error.

Educational data needs to be enriched, that is transformed into structured and formal descriptions by linking it to widely established Linked Data vocabularies and datasets on the web also linking these datasets in a efficient way in order to avoid redundancy.

In this context we found linksets from Nature.com, Educational Programs[16] and Geonames, in which such errors can be potentially detected by computing the closure of equivalence links using the characteristics of equivalence relations and an inference engine. In our case we are using CEDAL [VSN17a] which is the fastest and complete way to detect consistency errors.

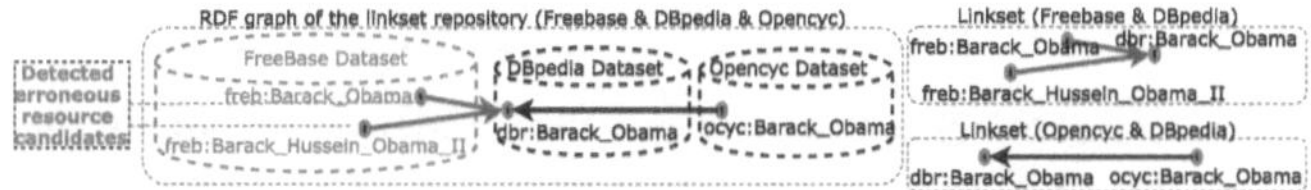

Figure 29: Manual detection of erroneous resource candidates.

5.3.2 Research questions

The research questions are:

- The link repositories from the educational area are consistent?

- Is there an approach to verify whether the links from educational area are consistent?

5.3.3 Our contributions

- An analysis of linksets from educational area.

- Applying CEDAL[VSN17a] in order to assess the consistency of linksets from educational area.

5.3.4 Evaluation

The evaluation shows the detected erroneous link candidates and fixing the linksets with problems.

Experimental setup

We evaluated our work using the datasets from Linked Education[17] listed in table 23, in which the main datasets are from *educational*

Programs[18] and dump-files[19] from Nature[20], where we used a sample of 1049 links.

Table 23: Educational Datasets

Dataset	State	number of transitive links
http://data.cnr.it/sparql	on-line	3907
http://meducator.open.ac.uk/resourcesrestapi/rest/meducator/sparql	off-line	
http://data.open.ac.uk/query	on-line	20956
http://asn.jesandco.org:8890/sparql	off-line	
http://services.data.gov.uk/education/sparql	off-line	
http://knowone.csc.kth.se/sparql/ariadne-big	off-line	
http://data.nature.com/sparql/	off-line	
http://seek.rkbexplorer.com/sparql/	off-line	

The CEDAL can be applied only to transitive properties, that are respective *skos:exactMatch*, *owl:sameAs* and *skos:equivalentClass*, in which according to the table 24 are a total of 1,046 links. All linkset files from were copied locally to run the experiments.

Table 24: Educational Linksets

Linkset (Source x Target)			
Source	**Target**	**Links (triples)**	**Type**
educationalPrograms	geonames	792	owl:sameAs
nature.com	dbpedia.org/resource	94	skos:exactMatch
nature.com	wikidata.org	92	skos:exactMatch
nature.com	schema.org	13	owl:equivalentClass
nature.com	purl.org	26	owl:equivalentClass
nature.com	cidoc-crm.org	10	owl:equivalentClass
nature.com	dbpedia.org/ontology	9	owl:equivalentClass
nature.com	xmlns.com	5	owl:equivalentClass
nature.com	vivoweb.org	5	owl:equivalentClass

The experiments were performed using a laptop with Intel Core i7, 8 GB RAM, a video card NVIDIA NVS4200, Operational System Linux Ubuntu 14.4 and Java SE Development Kit 8. The results including the output file are available on CEDAL online repository[21]. All links were processed by our algorithm in 190 milliseconds. The total amount of errors were 20 of candidates, with 2 different domains and 2 knowledge base files.

Ranking the erroneous candidates

To evaluate how effective CEDAL detect the erroneous links in educational linksets, CEDAL has a score in order to rank the erroneous candidates based on the number of detected resources with errors.

The score μ is calculated by $\mu = \frac{|C|(|C|-1)}{2}$, in which we use the cardinality of C representing the detected erroneous candidates.

The figure 30 shows the the number of erroneous candidates according the rank score.

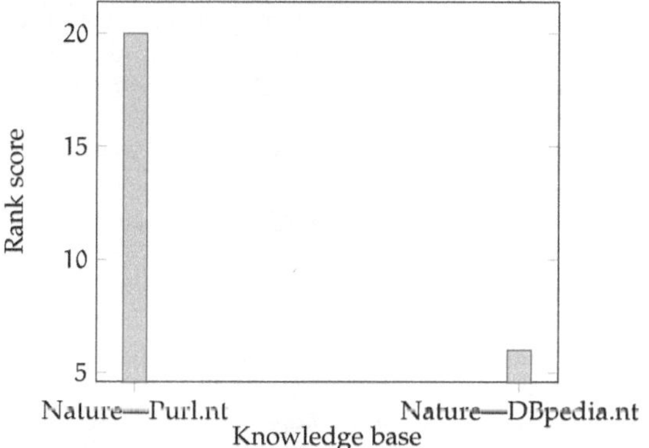

Figure 30: Error rank, where Nature—Purl.nt represent the file with links between Nature and Purl.org and Nature—DBpedia.nt represent the links between Nature and DBpedia

According to our rank, the knowledge-base with more errors comes from $npg - core - any - linkset.nq.nt - - - purl.org.nt$ with 25 links per mapping, in which we found 20 erroneous resource candidates. The knowledge base with fewer errors was $npg - journals - dbpedia - linkset.nq.nt - - - dbpedia.org.nt$ with 94 links per mapping, in which we found 6 erroneous resource candidates and a sum of score of 3.

Analyzing and Fixing the problems We use an example from CEDAL output file[22] to show how to fix a Linkset. Among the errors detected we choose the linkset file $npg - core - any - linkset.nq.nt$, in which has a case where 2 error candidates that are transitive and are in the same dataset. In this case, we have an error type 2, where the following resource is duplicated within the DBpedia dataset.

QUERYING LARGE AMOUNT OF HETEROGENEOUS RDF DATASETS

This chapter aims present the work related to the RQ6 [VSS19], which shows the approach about Querying a Large Amount of Heterogeneous RD Datasets.

In this chapter, we cover the RQ6 in which we discuss the fact that over the last years, the Web of Data has grown significantly. Various interfaces such as LOD Stats, LOD Laudromat, SPARQL endpoints provide access to the hundered of thousands of RDF datasets, representing billions of facts. These datasets are available in different formats such as raw data dumps and HDT files or directly accessible via SPARQL endpoints. Querying such large amount of distributed data is particularly challenging and many of these datasets cannot be directly queried using the SPARQL query language. In order to tackle these problems, we present WimuQ, an integrated query engine to execute SPARQL queries and retrieve results from large amount of heterogeneous RDF data sources. Presently, WimuQ is able to execute both federated and non-federated SPARQL queries over a total of 668,166 datasets from LOD Stats and LOD Laudromat as well as 559 active SPARQL endpoints. These data sources represent a total of 221.7 billion triples from more than 5 terabytes of information from datasets retrieved using the service "Where is My URI" (WIMU). Our evaluation on state-of-the-art real-data benchmarks shows that WimuQ retrieves more complete results for the benchmark queries.

6.1 INTRODUCTION

Currently, the LOD Laudromat along with LOD stats have more than 250 billion facts which are available on 668,166 datasets and 559 active SPARQL endpoints [VSN+18]. Querying such large amount of distributed data is particularly challenging in which Federated query processing is one of the key components for accessing this collection of information through these data sources. In general, there are two types of available approaches to execute federated SPARQL queries over distributed RDF data sources [SKH+15]. (1) Query federation over multiple SPARQL endpoints (QFME) which collects distributed information from multiple SPARQL endpoints. Commonly, the list of SPARQL endpoints is provided as an input to the federation engine. The federation engine decomposes the original query into multiple sub-queries and execute them accordingly to a specific query execution plan. (2) Link Traversal based SPARQL federation (LTSF) which uses the URI lookups to collect information from distributed RDF data sources. Such approaches do not force the data providers to publish their data as SPARQL endpoints. Instead, the only requirement is that the RDF data sources must follow the Linked Data principles[1] [Har13a].

However, a particular shortcoming of the QFME approaches is that many of the RDF datasets in Linking Open Data (LOD) are not publicly available via SPARQL endpoints. Beek et al. [BRB⁺14] has shown that around 90% of the information published are available only as data dumps. On the other hand, the LTSF approaches are unable to perform lookups for non-dereferenceable URIs. Hence, they may retrieve empty or incomplete results for the latter type of approaches. Note that our previous work [VSN⁺18] shows that around 43% of the URIs of more than 660K RDF datasets from LODStats [ELMA16] and LODLaundromat [BRB⁺14] are non-dereferenceable.

In this work, dubbed WIMU Query (wimuQ), we provide an approach that overcomes the limitations of the state of the art regarding to the coverage of the results. WimuQ is a hybrid (endpoints federation + link traversal) federated SPARQL query processing engine which collects distributed information from SPARQL endpoints as well as raw data dumps and HDT files [FMPG⁺13]. WimuQ integrates exciting state-of-the-art LTSF and QFME approaches into a single query execution framework. Additionally, WimuQ overcomes the problem of non-dereferenceable URIs by making use of our previous index of 4.2 billion URIs from more than 660k RDF datasets [VSN⁺18]. Our evaluation on state-of-the-art real-data benchmarks shows that WimuQ retrieves more complete results on three different benchmarks for federated SPARQL query engines [SGH⁺11; SMN15; SHN18].

The contributions of this paper are as follows:

- We present a hybrid SPARQL query processing engine which is is able to retrieve results from 559 active SPARQL endpoints (with a total of 163.23 billion triples) and 668,166 datasets (with a total of 58.49 billion triples) from LOD Stats and LOD Laundromat. Thus, to the best of our knowledge, WimuQ is the first federated SPARQL query processing engine that executes SPARQL queries over a net total of 221.7 billion triples

- As part of WimuQ, we present a low-cost API dubbed *SPARQL-a-lot* to execute SPARQL queries over LOD-a-lot [FBMPA17], a 300 GB HDT file of the LOD cloud. For the first time, to the best of our knowledge, we make use of the Concise Bounded Descriptions (CBDs), 4 to execute federate SPARQL queries.

- We make use of the WIMU index [VSN⁺18] to intelligently select the capable (also called relevant) [SNN14] data sources pertaining to the given SPARQL query. We evaluated our integrated query engine on two real-data federated SPARQL query-ing benchmarks *LargeRDFBench* [SHN16],*FedBench* [SGH+11] and one non-federated real data SPARQL benchmark selected from *FEASIBLE* [SMN15] benchmarks generation framework.

WimuQ is open source and available from along with complete evaluation results. The web ver-sion of the WimuQ is available from The rest of the chapter is organized as follows: WimuQ approach in section 6.3. Section **??** shows the evaluation results and discussion.

6.2 DEFINITIONS

Let **Q** be a SPARQL query and $\mathcal{D}$ be a finite set of the datasets which can be retrieved using WIMU [VSN+18]. For each data source $D \in \mathcal{D}$, we write $G(D)$ to denote the underlying RDF graph exposed by D. When requesting data source D to execute a SPARQL query Q, we expect that the result of D is the set $Q_{G(D)}$. Hence, we define the result set $S(\mathbf{Q})$ of a SPARQL query over the federation $\mathcal{D}$ to be a

set of solution mappings that is equivalent to $Q_{G(\mathcal{D})}$ where $G_{\mathcal{D}} = \bigcup_{D \in \mathcal{D}} G(D)$.

We formalize the problem in two steps as follows: (1) *find the datasets on which a given query can be executed* and (2) *return the query results from the selected datasets.*[2]

6.3 THE WIMUQ

In this section, we explain the WimuQ approach to the SPARQL query processing. We assume that the reader is familiar with the concepts of RDF and SPARQL, including the notions of an RDF triple, a triple pattern, a basic graph pattern (BGP), and subject, predicate, object of the triple pattern.

Figure 31 shows the workflow of the query processing in our ap-proach, which comprises of 7 main steps: (1) the user issue a SPARQL query to the WimuQ interface, which (2) extracts all the URIs used in the given user query. Note the URIs can be used in subject, pred-icate, or objects of the SPARQL triple patterns. (3) The extracted URIs are then searched in the WIMU index, which gives all the rel-evant datasets where the extracted URIs can be found. (4) Our Re-lational index *ReLOD*[AV20] will provide the most similar datasets, adding more relevant datasets and excluding nonrelevant datasets, (5) the relevant datasets are furthered filtered based on the source selection algorithm, and (6) the finally-selected relevant datasets are then queried by using the different query processors, depending on

---

2 Throughout the paper, we refer to RDF dump files or any datasets accessible using a SPARQL endpoint as *datasets*, *data sources* or simply *sources*.

the type (HDT, endpoint, datadump, dereferenceable dataset) of the datasets; (7) the results generated by the different query processors are then integrated and sent back to the user. The whole process is like a black box to the end user: the user only sends the query and get back the results without knowing the underlying query execution steps.

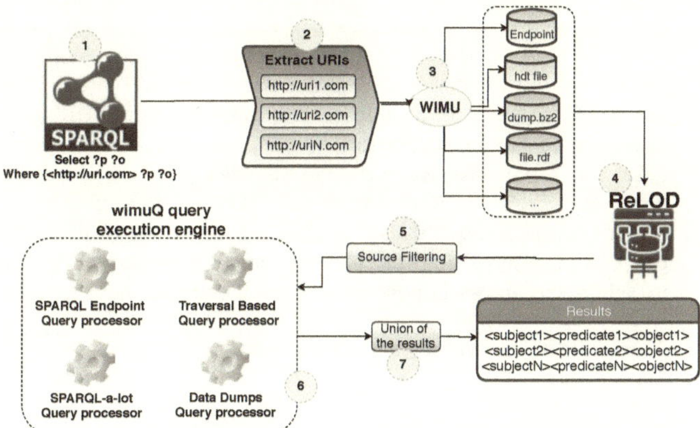

Figure 31: Query processing workflow, already including *ReLOD*[AV20]

Now we go into the details of these steps, explaining the different components.

6.3.1 *WimuQ source selection*

One of the important optimization steps in federated SPARQL query processing is the *source selection* [PSS+17; SNN14]. The goal of the source selection is to identify the potentially relevant datasets (also called sources) to the given query. We make use of the WIMU service [VSN+18] to select the potentially relevant sources. The WIMU service[3] provides URIs lookup facility and identify those datasets which contain the given URI. Currently, this service processed more than 58 billion unique triples and indexed 4.2 billion URIs from more than 66ok RDF datasets obtained from the most used Linked Data hubs including LODStats [ADML12] and LOD Laundromat [BRB+14]. The identified WIMU datasets can be of four types: (1) SPARQL endpoint, (2) HDT file, (3) dataset with dereferenceable URIs, (4) data dump with non-dereferenceable URIs. The service is both available from a web interface as well as can be queried from a client application using the standard HTTP protocol.

The WimuQ source selection algorithm is given in Algorithm 5 which takes a SPARQL query Q as input. We provide the set of extracted URIs (from step 2) U to the WIMU service and retrieve the relevant datasets D pertaining to the given URIs (Lines 1-4 of Algorithm 5). Now for each relevant dataset d $\in$ D, if the d is a SPARQL endpoint, we extract the individual triple patterns t of the query and perform a SPARQL ASK of t in dataset d (Lines 5-8 of Algorithm 5). We add the dataset d into the set of relevant SPARQL endpoints E, if the SPARQL ASK query returns true (Lines 9-13 of Algorithm 5). We directly add d into sets H and T if d is an HDT file or if the d is a SPARQL endpoint or dataset with dereferenceable URIs, respectively (Lines 14-19 of Algorithm 5). Finally, if d is dataset with non-dereferenceable URIs, we apply the RDFSlice [MSS$^+$17] technique to only get the relevant RDF slice of the dataset. The RDF slice is then considered as a relevant dataset (Lines 20-23 of Algorithm 5). The purpose of only adding the relevant slice of the complete dataset is to reduce the processing overhead, explained in the next section.

Algorithm 5 The WimuQ source selection

```
Input: Q                                              ▷ The SPARQL query
Output: E, H, T, N                          ▷ Hash sets of relevant sources
of SPARQL endpoints, HDT files, dataset with dereferenceable URIs, datadump with
non-dereferenceable URIs, respectively
 1: U = extractURIs(Q)              ▷ Extract the URIs from the SPARQL query
 2: for all u ∈ U do
 3:     D = D ∪ wimuLookup(u)                  ▷ Datasets from the WIMU
 4: end for
 5: for all d ∈ D do                                    ▷ For each dataset
 6:     if d is SPARQL endpoint then
 7:         for all t ∈ Q do            ▷ For each Triple pattern in query
 8:             b = ASK(t,d)                      ▷ SPARQL ASK of t in d
 9:             if b = true then
10:                 E.add(d)
11:             end if
12:         end for
13:     end if
14:     if d is HDT file then
15:         H.add(d)
16:     end if
17:     if d is dataset with dereferenceable URIs then
18:         T.add(d)
19:     end if
20:     if d is datadump with non-dereferenceable URIs then
21:         N.add(RDFSlice(d))                    ▷ only add the relevant slice
22:     end if
23: end for
24: return E, H, T, N                         ▷ final relevant sources set
```

6.3.2 *WimuQ query execution*

We make use of the four – SPARQL endpoint, Link Traversal-based, SPARQL-a-alot, Data dumps – query processor to execute federated queries over the aforementioned four types of WIMU datasets. The relevant data sources for each of these query processors are returned by the WimuQ source selection discussed in previous section.

In WimuQ, we used FedX [SHH+11] query processor for SPARQL endpoints query federation and SQUIN for traversal-based query federation. The reason for choosing FedX for SPARQL endpoints federation and SQUIN for traversal-based federation is due the fact that they do not require any pre-computation of dataset statistics and hence are able to retrieve up-to-date results. Thus both are able to run federated queries with zero initial knowledge. In addition, both produce reasonably query runtime performances comparing to state-of-the-art approaches [SKH+15; SPS+18; Har13b].

The list of required endpoints URLs for FedX are returned from the previously discussed source selection Algorithm (ref. **E** of Algorithm 5). The potentially relevant dereferenceable URIs data sources (ref. **T** of Algorithm 5) are already identified by the WimuQ sources selection algorithm. Thus, we reduced the search space by only considering the dereferenceable URIs data sources.

As mentioned before, FedX can only works with public SPARQL endpoints. SQUIN needs dereferenceable URIs. Both of these engines are unable to execute SPARQL queries over non-dereferenceable URIs datadumps: SPARQL endpoint federation approaches cannot execute queries over such datadumps as they are not exposed as SPARQL endpoints, link traversal-based approaches fail to retrieve results as the URIs are non-dereferenceable. We need to download the dumps first, load it locally, and run some query processing API (e.g., JENA or Sesame) on the loaded datasets. However, we can not simply download the complete dumps and process it locally due to their large amount of data. To solve this problem, we make use of the Wimu index to only select those data dumps which are potentially capable to execute the given query. These datadumps are further sliced by using the RDFSlice technique, to only select the required chunks of the datadumps which will provide results to the given SPARQL query. The identified chunks are finally loaded in a local Apache Jena model. The model is then use to execute federated queries.

Finally, we propose a query processor named *SPARQL-a-lot* to execute federated SPARQL queries over HDT files. The SPARQL-a-lot is a CBD-based[4] query execution described in Algorithm 6. The algorithm takes a SPARQL query Q as input and return the resultset O of the query execution over HDT file. First, the algorithm extracts all of the BGPs from Q (Line 2 of Algorithm 6). The next step is to extract the subjects, predicates, and objects of all the triple patterns used in Q (Line 3 of Algorithm 6). The CBDs are then generated from extracted subjects, predicates, and objects (Line 4 of Algorithm 6). The extracted CBDs constitute an RDF dataset of set of triples T which are then loaded into a local Jena model (Line 5 of Algorithm 6). The query Q is then finally executed over the Jena model and results are returned (Lines 6-7 of Algorithm 6). The duplicated results from different query processing engines is removed after collecting the final results.

Algorithm 6 Query execution on LOD-a-lot

Input: Q   ▷ The SPARQL query
Output: O   ▷ The results of the query

1: **procedure** SPARQL-A-LOT(**Q**)
2:    **BGP** = extractBGP(**Q**)   ▷ Extract the BGP from the SPARQL query
3:    **Tbgp** = extractSPO(**BGPs**)
4:    **T** = executeAPILOD-a-LOT(**Tbgp**)   ▷ Generating CBDs from s, p, o
5:    createTDBJena(**T**)
6:    **O** = execSPARQLTDBJena(**Q**)
7:    return **O**
8: **end procedure**

The results generated by each of WimuQ's processors are finally integrated and sent back to the user.

6.3.3 *Practical example*

Given the following SPARQL query (LD1 from FEDBench[SGH$^+$11]):

```
1  PREFIX rdfs: <http://www.w3.org/2000/01/rdf-schema#>
2  SELECT * WHERE { ?paper
3  <http://data.semanticweb.org/ns/swc/ontology#isPartOf>
4  <http://data.semanticweb.org/conference/iswc/2008/
5  poster_demo_proceedings> .
6  ?paper <http://swrc.ontoware.org/ontology#author> ?p .
7  ?p rdfs:label ?n .
8  }
```

With WimuQ we were able to identify 4 HDT datasets available from . All of these datasets are from LOD Laundromat repository [BRB$^+$14] containing information about the conference ISWC2008 [SSD$^+$08], under the domain originally from SW Dog Food dataset[5]. Thus, *SPARQL-a-lot* is the only query processing engine (because of the selected datasets are HDTs) which is considered for executing the given SPARQL queries. The final results of the query execution is available.

6.4   EVALUATION

In this section, we present the evaluation setup and the corresponding results that validate our hypothesis that we can improve the result-set retrieval if we automatically identify potentially relevant sources from heterogeneous RDF data even if the URIs are not dereference-able anymore. The goal of this evaluation is to show that by combining different SPARQL query processing approaches, we are able to retrieve more complete results as compared to the results retrieved by the individual approaches.

6.4.1   *Experimental setup*

Benchmarks used:

Since WimuQ aims to execute SPARQL queries over real-world RDF datasets, we chose three – FedBench [SGH$^+$11], LargeRDFBench [SHN16], Feasible [SMN15] – real-world RDF datasets benchmarks in our evaluation:

- **FedBench** is federated SPARQL querying benchmarks. It comprises of a total of 25 queries and 9 real-world interconnected datasets. FedBench queries are further divided into three main categories: (1) 7 queries from Life Sciences (LS) domain, (2) 7 queries from Cross Domain (CD), and (3) 11 queries named Linked Data (LD) for link traversal-based approaches. The detailed statistics of the benchmark's datasets and queries are given in FedBench[SGH$^+$11].

- **LargeRDFBench** is also a federated SPARQL querying benchmark. It comprises a total of 40 queries and 13 real-world interconnected datasets. FedBench queries are further divided into four main categories: (1) 14 *Simple* queries, (2) 10 *Complex* queries, (3) 8 *Large Data* queries, and (4) 8 *Complex+High Data Sources* queries. The detailed statistics of the benchmark's datasets and queries are given in [SHN16].

- **FEASIBLE** is a benchmark generation framework which generates customized benchmarks for the queries logs. In our evaluation, we chose exactly the same benchmarks used in [SMN15]: (1) 175 queries benchmark generated from DBpedia queries log and (2) 175 queries benchmark generated from Semantic Web Dog Food (SWDF) queries log. Further advanced statistics of the used datasets and queries can be found in [SMN15].

To the best of our knowledge, these are the state-of-the-art from the real-data SPARQL benchmarks. All of the 415 queries used in our evaluation is publicly available[6].

Hardware:

All the experiments were done on a modest machine with 200 GB of Hard Disk, 8 GB of RAM and a 2.70GHz single core processor. Each of the queries was run 5 times and the average of the results are presented.

SPARQL endpoints:

As previously stated, the query federation over multiple SPARQL endpoints approaches requires the set of endpoint URLs to be provided as input to the federation engine. We chose a total of 539 active SPARQL endpoints available from LOD cloud[7]. We filtered the endpoints URLs[8] and the total number of triples hosted by each of these endpoints.

Metrics:

Since WimuQ aims to retrieve more complete results within the reasonable amount of time, we choose two metrics: (1) coverage in terms of the number of results retrieved from the query executions and (2) the time taken to execute the benchmark queries.

Approaches:

As mentioned in Section 3, different federation engines available to federate SPARQL queries over endpoints and traversal-based federation. We chose FedX [SHH+11] for SPARQL endpoint federation and SQUIN [Har13b] for traversal-based query federation. The reason for choosing these two engines is due the fact they do not require any pre-computation of dataset statistics and hence able to retrieve up-to-date results and able to run federated queries with zero initial knowledge. In addition, both these engines perform reasonably well in terms of query runtime performances w.r.t state-of-the-art approaches [SKH+15; SPS+18; Har13b]. For the sake of completeness, we also compared WimuQ with SPARQL-a-lot and WimuDumps.

6.4.2 *Results*

Coverage of the results: The main purpose of WimuQ is to devise a federation engine which is able to retrieve more complete results for the given SPARQL queries. figure 32 shows a comparison of the selected approaches in terms of the average of the number of results retrieved for the different queries categories of the selected benchmarks. The complete results for individual queries can be found on our aforementioned project website. By using different query processing engines, our approach is able to retrieve more results as compared to the results retrieved by only using SPARQL endpoints federation engine (i.e, FedX) link traversal engine (i.e., SQUIN), data dumps, or HDT files. In our evaluation, the average resultset size of WimuQ is 8481 across the three benchmarks. Out of these, WimuQ collects about 91% of the results from wimuDumps (avg. resultset size 7651), 7% from SPARQL endpoints (avg. resultset size 556), and 1% from SPARQL-a-lot (avg. resultset size 74).

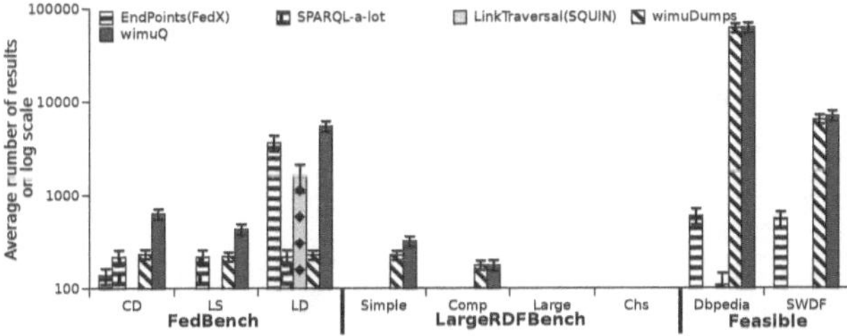

Figure 32: Average number of results retrieved by the selected approaches across different queries categories of the selected benchmarks.

For FedBench, the WimuQ avg. resultset size is 2,253. Out of these results, about 55% are collected from SPARQL endpoints by using FedX query processing engines (avg. resultset size 1,262). The Link-Traversal (SQUIN) contributed about 25% of the total results (avg. resultset size 549), wimuDumps contributed about 10% of the total results (avg. resultset size 226), and SPARQL-a-lot also contributed about 10% of the results (avg. resultset size 215).

For LargeRDFBench, the WimuQ avg. resultset size 123. Out of these results, about 81% are collected from wimuDumps (avg. resultset size 100). The SPARQL endpoints contributed about 14% of the results (avg. resultset size 17). The LinkTraversal(SQUIN) contributed 6% of the total results (avg. resultset size 6), and SPARQL-a-lot did not provide results (avg. resultset size 0).

For FEASIBLE, the WimuQ avg. resultset size 34,537. Out of these results, about 98% are collected from wimuDumps (avg. resultset size 33,893). The SPARQL endpoints contributed about 1.6% (avg. resultset size 577). The LinkTraversal(SQUIN) approach contributed only about 0.15% (avg. resultset size 54). Finally, SPARQL-a-lot query processing engine only retrieved about 0.03% results (avg. resultset size 11).

In summary, WimuQ is able to retrieve at least one resultset for 76% of the overall 415 queries. The results clearly shows that by combining different query processing engines into a single SPARQL query execution framework lead towards more complete resultset retrieval. An important observation is that the selected approaches are mostly not able to retrieve results for the Large Data and Complex+High (Ch) queries categories of LargeRDFBench. The reason is getting zero results for the Large Data queries is that these queries retrieve results from the LinkedTCGA [SPN⁺13b] datasets which were not publicly available via SPARQL endpoints, were not indexed by WIMU, also were not reachable via link traversals. While Ch queries often require higher number of distributed datasets in order to compute the final resultset of the queries. Thus, the approaches were able to find all of the relevant datasets, required to compute the final resultset of the queries. The average number of datasets[9] queries by WimuQ for the selected benchmarks queries categories in given in Figure 33. We can clearly see the highest number of datasets are selected for Ch queries of LargeRDFBench.

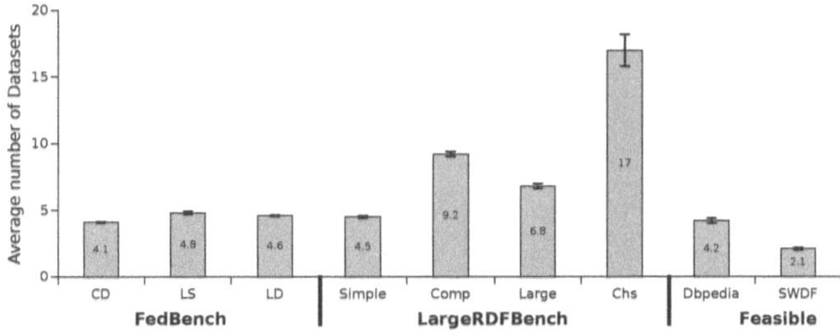

Figure 33: Average number of datasets discovered and queried by WimuQ across different queries categories of the selected benchmarks.

Query runtime performances: figure 34 shows a comparison of the selected query processing engines in terms of the average query run times for the different queries categories of the selected benchmarks. The average query runtime of WimuQ is 17 minutes across the three benchmarks. The average query execution to collect results from wimuDumps is about 2 minutes, which in turn is followed by query execution over SPARQL endpoints (avg. query runtime 13 minutes), SPARQL-a-lot (avg. query runtime 58 seconds) and LinkTraversal (SQUIN) (avg. query runtime 36 seconds). Interestingly, WimuQ collects about 91% of the results from wimuDumps yet its average execution time is smaller than query execution over SPARQL endpoints

---

9 Here we also point the number of datasets discovered

which provide only 7% of the total results. One possible reason for this could be that in SPARQL endpoint federation, the query processing task split among multiple selected SPARQL endpoints and hence network and the number of intermediate results play an important role in the quer runtime performances.

For FedBench, the WimuQ average query runtime 20 minutes. Out of this, the average avg. query runtime over SPARQL endpoints is 16 minutes, followed by wimuDumps (avg. query runtime 2 minutes), LinkTraversal (SQUIN) (avg. query runtime 49 seconds), and SPARQL-a-lot (avg. query runtime 46 seconds), respectively. For LargeRDFBench, the average query execution of WimuQ is 11 minutes. Out of this query execution over SPARQL endpoints took 8 minuts on average, followed by wimuDumps (avg. query runtime 2 minutes), SPARQL-a-lot (avg. query runtime 35 seconds), and Link-Traversal (SQUIN) (avg. query runtime 25 seconds), respectively. For FEASIBLE, the WimuQ takes on average of 24 minutes per query execution. Out of this, the query federation over SPARQL endpoints took about 18 minutes on average. Which is followed by wimuDumps (avg. query runtime 3 minutes), SPARQL-a-lot (avg. query runtime 1), and LinkTraversal (SQUIN) (avg. query runtime 36 seconds), respectively.

As an overall query runtime evaluation, we can clearly see there is a trade-off between the recall and query runtimes: the highest the recall the highest the query runtimes. Finding a balance between the recall and runtime would be an interesting research question to be considered in the future.

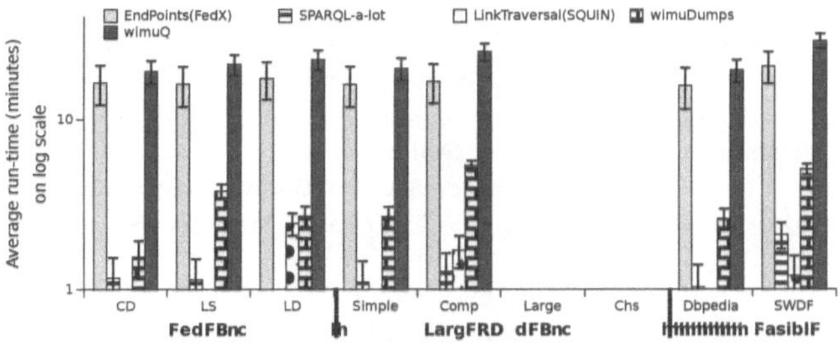

Figure 34: Average query runtimes of the selected approaches across different queries categories of the selected benchmarks.

The results of our evaluation lead us to validate our hypothesis that we can improve the resultset retrieval if we identify potentially relevant sources from heterogeneous RDF data.

CONCLUSION AND FUTURE WORK

Here we conclude the book presenting the answers to the research questions and the future works.

7.1 IDENTIFYING DATASETS IN LARGE HETEROGENEOUS RDF SOURCES

To answer the research question RQ1, based on the evaluation 4.1.4 we provide a database index of URIs and their respective datasets built upon large Linked Data hubs such as LODStats and LOD Laundromat. In order to make this data available and easy to use, we developed a semantic web service. For a given URI, it is possible to know the dataset the URI likely was defined in using a heuristic based on the number of literals. We showed two use-cases and carried out a preliminary evaluation to facilitate the understanding of our work. As future work, we will integrate the service into the version 2.0 of the LinkLion repository, so as to perform linkset quality assurance with the application of link discovery algorithms on the stored links.

7.2 RELATING LARGE AMOUNT OF RDF DATASETS

To answer the research question RQ2, based on the evaluation 4.2.3 we present a method to create a repository to store the similarity between a large number of datasets involving the detection of duplicated datasets and dataset chunks.

The method involves the creation of an index over a total of 668,166 datasets from LOD Stats and LOD Laundromat as well as 559 active SPARQL endpoints, representing a total of 221.7 billion triples from more than 5 terabytes of information from datasets partially retrieved using the service "Where is My URI" (WIMU).

For the first time, to the best of our knowledge, we make a relation index that can query by dataset URI, property, class, or SPARQL query.

Our experiments show that more than 90% of datasets from LODLaundromat datasets are not using owl:equivalentProperty and owl:equivalentClass or another way to relate the data, reinforcing the need for an index of relations among LOD datasets.

We realize that the Datasets still not sharing the expected properties, and the ontologies are not aligned, making hard the task to query multiple heterogeneous datasets. We believe that this work can help people to identify similar datasets among a large number of datasets. As future work, the next step is to improve the GUI drawing a weighted graph that shows the similarity level of each dataset. The source-code is available online[1].

7.3 OBTAINING SIMILAR RESOURCES USING STRING SIMILARITY

To answer the research question RQ3, based on the evaluation 4.3.4 we presented an approach to reduce the computation runtime of similarity joins using the Most Frequent k Characters algorithm with a sequence of filters that allow discarding pairs before computing their actual similarity, thus reducing the runtime of computation. We proved that our approach is both correct and complete. The evaluation shows that all filter setup outperform the naive approach. Our parallel implementation works better in larger datasets with size greater than 10^5 pairs. It is also the key to developing systems for Record Linkage and Link Discovery in knowledge bases. As future work, we plan to integrate it in link discovery applications for the validation of equivalence links. The source code is free and available online.[2]

7.4 HETEROGENEITY IN DBPEDIA IDENTIFIERS

To answer the research question RQ4, based on the evaluation 5.1.5 an approach was provided to tackle the heterogeneity working with `owl:sameAs` redundancies that were observed during researching co-references between different data sets and providing a unique DBpedia identifier and give the chance to rate the resulting links and make suggestions.

A proof of concept was implemented as a computer web system in order to present and validate our idea and every concept of this work. The source code is available [3].

Was noticed in our results that there are benefits when a considerable number of `owl:sameAs` redundancies can be avoided. Rating the links allow users to make link suggestions brings more quality to the repository, and the stand alone service on the web allow you to use the DBpediaSameAs also in a command line textual environment and can be used as an off-the-shelf component.

For the future we plan to: (1) make a study about the results of link rating. This needs a period of usage of the DBpediaSameAs service in order to gather sufficient results for proper analysis. (2) An implementation case with more members of the DBpedia community.

A study about how will be the behavior when implement with the DBpedia community.

7.5   DETECTION OF ERRONEOUS LINKS IN LARGE-SCALE RDF DATASETS

In this work, evaluated in 5.2.4 we answer the RQ5 and we present CEDAL, a new algorithm that allows tracking consistency problems inside linkset repositories. Our approach allows detecting potential causes of errors, for example the linkset, the underlying dataset(s) and the graph path where the problem subsists. We showed that our approach scales well. In particular, we reduced the complexity of obtaining clusters by relying on graph partitions, thus decreasing the time complexity from $O(n^2)$ to $O(m \log n)$. Our results showed that at least 13% of owl:sameAs links we considered are erroneous, and algorithms LIMES, SILK and DBpedia Extraction Framework have a better consistency index than repositories such as *sameas.org*.

In future work, we will carry out a survey on Linkset quality. To the best of our knowledge, the survey [ZRM⁺15] is the most complete collection of data quality measures, which, however, misses specific measures for linkset quality, such as ways a linkset can improve dataset quality [AP13; YKB15; CVL⁺14]. Moreover, we will investigate how our graph partition algorithms can improve the performance of SPARQL endpoints by distributing resources among computer clusters, core processors, and GPUs. The CEDAL repository[4] contains all necessary resources to run CEDAL, verify and reproduce our results.

7.6   DETECTING ERRONEOUS LINK CANDIDATES IN EDUCATIONAL LINK REPOSITORIES

In this part of the conclusions, we use an approach dubbed CEDAL[VSN17a] in order to assess consistency problems inside linkset repositories from the educational area. CEDAL allows detecting potential causes of errors, for example, the linkset, the underlying dataset(s) and the graph path where the problem subsists. To evaluate the approach, we selected 1049 transitive links using datasets from Nature.com and Educational Programs. Our results showed that 20 links we considered are erroneous. We show a scenario where is possible to see how fragile is the educational linked data and a way to improve it detecting consistency problems. As future work we will apply this approach to more educational linked data, extend CEDAL to work with more link types and provide a usability study.

7.7   QUERYING LARGE HETEROGENEOUS RDF DATASETS

To answer the research question RQ6, we presented an approach to execute SPARQL queries over a large amount of heterogeneous RDF data sources available from different interfaces and in different formats, evaluated in 6.4. We made use of the Wimu service to identify the potentially relevant sources to the qiven SPARQL query. We discussed two main types of federated SPARQL query processing approaches namely the endpoints federation and traversal-based federation. The former type of federation only able to execute federated queries over the data available from SPARQL endpoint. While the later, faces problem of URI's dereferenceability. To overcome these issues we proposed a hybrid (endpoints+link-traversal-based) federation engines which integrates four different types of SPARQL query processing engines. Currently, WimuQ able to execute both federated and non-federated SPARQL queries over a total of 668k datasets available from LOD Stats, LOD Laudromat, and LOD cloud active SPARQL endpoints. We evaluated WimuQ by using three state-of-the-art real-data SPARQL benchmarks. We showed that WimuQ is able to successful execute (with some results) majority of the benchmark queries without any prior knowledge of the data sources. In addition, the WimuQ resultset recall is higher with reasonable query execution times.

As future, we will add more URIs into the the WIMU index in order to retrieve more complete and fast results. Furthermore, we will add TPF interfaces and query execution engines such Comunica [TVHVSV18] and SAGE [MSM18] into the WimuQ query execution engine. We will continue maintaining[5] and developing, extending WimuQ to include the publicly-available triple pattern fragments interfaces as well[6].

9 783384 230041